Achieving Emotional Literacy

Other Books by Claude Steiner

Games Alcoholics Play
Scripts People Live
The Warm Fuzzy Tale
Beyond Games and Scripts
Readings in Radical Psychiatry
The Other Side of Power
Healing Alcoholism
When a Man Loves a Woman

ACHIEVING
EMOTIONAL
LITERACY

A Personal Program
to Increase Your
Emotional Intelligence

Claude Steiner, Ph.D.
with Paul Perry

AVON BOOKS NEW YORK

AVON BOOKS
A division of
The Hearst Corporation
1350 Avenue of the Americas
New York, New York 10019

Copyright © 1997 by Claude M. Steiner and Paul Perry
Interior design by Kellan Peck
Visit our website at **http://AvonBooks.com**
ISBN: 0-380-97591-2

Library of Congress Cataloging in Publication Data:

Steiner, Claude, 1935–
    Achieving emotional literacy : a personal program to increase your
emotional intelligence / Claude Steiner ; with Paul Perry. — 1st
ed.
        p. cm.
    Includes bibliographical references and index.
    1. Emotions. I. Perry, Paul, 1950– . II. Title.
BF531.S814 1997   97-22834
152.4—dc21   CIP

First Avon Books Printing: November 1997

AVON TRADEMARK REG. U.S. PAT. OFF. AND IN OTHER COUNTRIES, MARCA
REGISTRADA, HECHO EN U.S.A.

Printed in the U.S.A.

FIRST EDITION

QPM   10   9   8   7   6   5   4   3   2   1

To my mother
Valery,
whose heart I longed to touch

ACKNOWLEDGMENTS

This book is the culmination of twenty years of work. Literally hundreds of people have been involved in minor and major ways.

Thanks are due, first and foremost, to Eric Berne for taking me on as a disciple and teaching me most of what I know as a psychotherapist.

More than any book I have written before, this book was the result of very closely knit teamwork. Thanks to Jude Hall, my editorial assistant, who, besides editing these pages through many versions and revisions, has added examples, elaborations, and ideas, made my language richer, and acted as my intellectual and philosophical conscience as this work took shape.

Thanks are due to Nat Sobel for being the first of a score of agents I approached with this project to visualize a book that could find a mass market and for shepherding the writing process from beginning to end. His and Laura Nolan's suggestions and influence permeate this book.

Thanks to Paul Perry who, to prepare himself to co-write this book, read everything I have written, immersed himself in my life, and then produced a first draft upon which to hang the many changes that have been made since. His genius for extracting the essential elements of my work gave this book its present, hopefully accessible form and structure.

A very special thanks to Fred Jordan, who was my editor at Grove Press many years ago, now executive director at Fromm International Publishing Corporation. He has been available, one simple phone call away, to give invaluable advice in the proposal, negotiation, and writing stages of the book. I consider myself blessed to have such a wise and kind maven on my team. I also thank Ron Levaco and Charles Rappleye, who in a similar capacity gave sage advice at some of the strategic crossroads of this book's journey.

Thanks to Deirdre English and Gail Rebuck, who steadfastly supported my writing for many years before this book found an agent and a publisher. Thanks to Beth Roy, Mimi Steiner, Rod Coots, Bruce Carrol, Ron Levaco, and Saul Schultheis-Gerry for their reading of and many comments on the final manuscript, and to Ramona Ansolabehere, Charles Rappleye, and Michael Hanigan for useful critical commentary on the text. Adriane Rainer's reading, informed by many hours of previous editoral work on this material, was especially useful.

Also on the team, Ann McKay Thoroman, my editor at Avon Books, took an immediate liking to this book and persevered with unflagging interest and hard work. She gave the book several critical readings and was completely available when needed, frequently holding my hand with great kindness when, occasionally, the going got tough.

Thanks are due to all the people who over the years attended my seminars, workshops, and group and individual therapy, and all my friends and relatives, who shared their life experiences with me and provided the information upon which to base the assertions I make in this book. This is particularly true of my close family and their spouses; my children Noemi, Eric, and Denali, my brother Miguel, my sister Katy, and finally Jude Hall, my fiancée and editorial assistant, who for months was on hand at a moment's notice to brainstorm or labor on a portion of text or for whatever I needed to keep me going while bringing this book to completion.

In particular I want to thank the many emotional warriors around the globe, among them Marc Devos, Becky Jenkins, Ron Hurst, Denton Roberts, Beth Roy, Hartmut Oberdieck, Noemi Steiner, and Elisabeth Cleary.

Going back to the 1960s when these ideas were born, thanks

are due to Nancy Graham for first uttering the term "emotional literacy," which I promptly scooped up and have used ever since. I thank Hogie Wyckoff for helping shape the concepts of Pig Parent (now the Critical Parent) and the Stroke Economy. Hogie was also the first to insist that honesty was an essential component of a cooperative life style. Bob Schwebel deserves thanks for introducing cooperation to my thinking, and Marshall Rosenberg was the first to point out the importance of linking actions with feelings.

Thanks are due to all the members of the RAP Center in Berkeley who contributed their lives and ideas to the theories presented in this book, in particular to Becky Jenkins, Carmen Kerr, Hogie Wyckoff, Robert Schwebel, Joy Marcus, Rick de Golia, Sarah Winter, and those who joined us later, Sandy Spiker, Eric Moore, Darca Nicholson, Melissa Farley, Mark Weston, Marion Oliker, JoAnn Costello, Beth Roy, Randy Dunigan, and Barbara Moulton.

Finally, I thank David Geiseinger for pointing out that a relationship is as good as its dialogue, Chris Moore for informing me on the latest philosophical arguments about the nature of truth, and Marc Devos for suggesting that emotional literacy training could be divided into three stages: an opening of the heart, a gathering of information, and taking of responsibility.

CONTENTS

Achieving Emotional Literacy

INTRODUCTION

We have all heard dramatic stories of redemption: the once-hopeless alcoholic who is now clean and sober and spares no effort on behalf of the addicted, the reformed wife beater who now works to support women's shelters, or the greedy capitalist who has become a world-class philanthropist and proponent of business ethics. My story is much the same. I started as an extreme case of emotional retardation and today I make it my life's work to study the emotions and teach emotional literacy.

Growing up in Mexico City, I was raised to be a traditional European male. I ignored not only my own emotions, but the emotions of others with whom I came into contact. Looking back, I would say that many of the things I did were insensitive and hurtful to the people in my life. To make matters worse, I was educated as a scientist, a discipline that encourages detachment and rationality uncluttered by emotion. You might think that I decided to study psychology because I was interested in people's feelings. In fact my interest in psychology had to do with the belief that it would give me power over people;

to be in a position to help, but also to dominate.

As part of my training as a psychologist I had to learn to run a wire down the backbone of live frogs to destroy their spinal cords. As I performed this grisly task I told myself that it was important to suppress my feelings of horror if I wanted to be a real scientist.

Later on I participated in experiments in which rats were starved to learn about their responses to severe hunger. As a result of this training, I became doubly uninterested in my own feelings and the feelings of others. I was, I'm sad to say, particularly oblivious to the feelings of the women in my life.

What was this state of deep emotional illiteracy like? Looking back, I see myself as someone who had infatuations but no real attachments, who had little respect, regret, or guilt when it came to the way I treated others. I never felt sustained joy, and I never remembered any of my dreams. I never cried. Although I have a respectable IQ, when I look back at myself I see an emotional imbecile, a young man with a very low EQ.

Today I can say that I have truly come a long way from my dismal beginnings. I was introduced to my emotions—or should I say I stumbled upon them—in the late 1960s. Like an explorer discovering an exotic land, I was amazed and captivated by the emotional landscape within and around me. Eventually I decided to make emotions the subject of ongoing inquiry in my psychological practice. I am still on a quest to understand emotions. Although much about human feelings is still unclear to me, I find this quest honorable, full of pleasure, and above all empowering in my personal and working relationships.

EMOTIONS AND PERSONAL POWER

In modern society, power is generally thought of as control, mainly the ability to control people and/or money. When we think of a powerful person, for example, we picture a captain of industry or a shrewd politician, but we rarely think of a woman. We see a superstar athlete, like a baseball or basketball player, one who commands millions in salary, drives an exquisite car, and dates supermodels. We may picture the powerful as emotionally cool: the suave Donald Trump, the unflappable William Buckley, the easygoing and collected Michael Jordan, the arrogant Charles Barkley. People like these, with their impressive physical control and emotional detachment, are who we have come to equate with power.

Most of us never attain that kind of power and may not even be interested in it. But most of us do want to have the kind of personal power that is derived from satisfying relationships and fruitful work.

Emotional Literacy is a vital component of personal power. All too often in today's world our interactions are fraught with cynicism and easily become alarming and debilitating. The repeated experience of interpersonal failure is a source of hopelessness and depression. But when our interactions at home, with friends, on the street and at work are promising and mutually satisfying we feel encouraged and optimistic. Our enjoyment of life, our will to struggle, and our level of energy improve; in short, we feel empowered. Rather than guaranteeing access to unlimited cash and things, Emotional Literacy makes it possible that every conversation, every human contact, every partnership, however brief or long-term, yields the largest possible rewards for all involved.

When becoming emotionally literate, a person learns that emotions can bestow power on people. Emotional Literacy is the key to personal power because emotions *are* powerful. If you can make them work for you rather than against you they will empower you.

So what happened in my life that put me in touch with my emotions? Change came through my encounters and subsequent relationships with two different people seven years apart: a rogue psychiatrist and a feminist partner. Both these encounters were the kind in which two people reach across a gap and somehow connect deeply at first sight.

3

FINDING MY TEACHER

The first person who changed my life was Eric Berne, a forty-five-year-old psychiatrist. Berne had recently terminated his training as a psychoanalyst because of differences with his training analyst. He had been investigating some radical departures from psychoanalysis that would later be known as Transactional Analysis (TA).

In 1958 he started holding weekly meetings with a small group of devotees at his apartment a few blocks from San Francisco's Chinatown.

I was taken to one of these meetings by a friend. I found what Berne had to say very interesting and joined in the lively discussion. After the meeting, Berne asked me to return the next week, and I did. I rarely missed these meetings from then on until Berne died in 1971. I became Berne's disciple and learned everything he had to teach about his evolving theory.

Transactional Analysis is a technique that investigates human relationships by focusing on the precise content of people's interactions. TA is a simple yet powerful way of analyzing how people deal with each other and how they can change their lives by correcting their behavioral mistakes. This was a sharp departure from traditional psychoanalysis, which focuses on what goes on *inside* of people instead of *between* them. But the most radical idea of Berne's was that you could actually cure people of their emotional problems by showing them *how to act differently* with each other in their social transactions, rather than by helping them to understand *why* they were emotionally disturbed.

Because of his interest in social transactions, I learned from Berne how to listen to what people say to each other. I also learned how to use my intuition to uncover the emotions that people hide and to better understand what they really think and feel.

However, emotions were not, at the time, our focus. In fact, we saw them as being largely irrelevant to our work, which was simply studying interpersonal dealings from a rational perspective. Yet Berne's concepts had everything to do with the eventual development of Emotional Literacy training. For one, Berne developed the concept of the inner "Natural Child," discussed later in this book, which is the source of our emotional lives.

Berne discovered in each person three parts, which he called the Child, the Parent, and the Adult. He called these three parts of the normal personality *ego states*, and he believed that we acted as one of them at any given time.

You can learn about the ego states in one of the many books written about Transactional Analysis. Suffice it to say, the Child is the creative and emotional part of the self, the Adult is a rational "human computer," and the Parent is composed of a set of attitudes about people and life that function in us as if they were prerecorded tapes.

Berne taught us to pay close attention to the "social transactions" between people, especially which of the three ego states was involved. Transactional Analysis holds that you can learn everything you need to know about a person by watching the interactions of his or her ego states.

Another very important concept developed by Berne was something he called "strokes." Even though strokes can be positive or negative, a "stroke," in the way that we will use the term in this book, refers to a positive stroke, a show of affection. When you say to someone, "I like the way you look today," you are giving that person a stroke. By the same token, when you lovingly pat your child on the back or listen carefully to what your partner is saying, you are giving him or her a stroke. Strokes can be physical or verbal and are defined as the basic unit of human recognition. The kinds of strokes that people give and take are especially informative. Some people exchange mostly negative strokes and their lives are very different from those who manage to live on a diet of positive loving strokes.

These concepts formed the theoretical foundation of what was, for me, the next step: the transactional analytic study of emotions, or Emotional Literacy.

FORCED TO FEEL

I would never have made the connection between Transactional Analysis and Emotional Literacy were it not for another life-changing relationship. This relationship began in 1969 and plunged me into the world of feelings. Almost overnight I became deeply involved with a feminist—Hogie Wyckoff—who for the next seven years taught me the essentials of emotionality. Basically, she demanded that I "come out" emotionally: that I be honest about my feelings, that I ask for what I want, and above all that I learn to say "I love you" from the heart.

None of these demands was easy for me to meet. In fact, they were excruciatingly difficult. Under her loving, watchful tutelage, however, I made great emotional strides. It was exhausting work for her and in the end she could endure it no longer, but she left me a changed man.

I met Hogie while teaching a course in Radical Psychiatry at the Free University in Berkeley. Eventually the two of us (and others whom I mention in the Acknowledgments) established a RAP Center at the Berkeley Free Clinic. RAP stood for "Radical Approach to Psychiatry."

PRACTICING WHAT I LEARNED

We started a number of "contact" groups, in which participants were taught the principles of Transactional Analysis as it applied to cooperative relationships. The most popular contact group to evolve from this work was called "Stroke City: A Liberated Space for the Free Expression of Love." We began to develop the techniques for learning emotional literacy in "Stroke City." These techniques are designed to open the heart and are described in chapter 5.

Three times a week "Stroke City" gathered in a large room at the RAP Center.

In this room between four and six people could give

strokes, accept strokes, ask for strokes, even give themselves strokes. The leader of the group scrutinized every transaction. It was his or her job to make sure that people gave each other positive strokes rather than criticism, make sure they were wanted and accepted, and when needed, help the participants correct their transactions.

We created these early meetings to teach people to be loving and cooperative in a competitive and harsh world. We soon observed an unexpected side effect. Participants would often look around after a couple of hours and declare that they "loved everyone in the room." Virtually everyone left with the glow of affection on their faces and a light step. It became clear that these exercises had an effect on the participants' loving emotions. They were the foundation of what eventually developed into emotional literacy training.

CRITICAL PARENT DISCOVERED

During these "Stroke City" sessions we discovered the pervasive activity of the Critical Parent. The Critical Parent (the "Pig Parent" as we called it in those days) is the internal oppressor, that voice in our heads that keeps us from thinking good thoughts about ourselves and others.

For instance, when some of the participants tried to give or accept positive strokes, they would literally hear "voices in their heads" that told them why the strokes should not be given or taken. They told the participants, in either subtle or overt ways, that they were stupid, bad, or crazy for participating in this strange exercise.

We came to discover that virtually everyone has some kind of ruthless internal bully making him feel bad about himself. Although Berne associated this internal adversary with the Parent ego state, the Critical Parent does not necessarily have anything to do with our mothers or fathers. In fact, it is a composite of all the put-downs that we received as children as people tried to control and manipulate us. It's important to remember that the Critical Parent is like a tape recording of other people's thoughts and opinions and that it can be turned down or off and can virtually be removed from our lives alltogether.

Even though people need positive strokes to thrive, it became clear that when they tried to give, ask for, or accept strokes, they often had a severe crisis of self-esteem sometimes fueled by extreme anxiety and even self-loathing.

Some people hear a voice saying, "You're selfish. You don't deserve strokes," or "This is stupid, you'll make a fool of yourself; shut up"; others just feel anxious or self-conscious every time they give or ask for a stroke. Almost everyone has an internal bully who slanders him or her from time to time, especially when he or she is emotionally vulnerable. Part of the work of "Stroke City"—and Emotional Literacy—is to recognize and wrestle down the Critical Parent which not only attacks our self-esteem but also the self-esteem of people around us when we apply to them the same criticism our Critical Parent applies to us.

Our experience in "Stroke City" provided me with many insights into the nature of emotional life. One was that even though most people enjoyed "Stroke City" and wound up feeling good, there were always a few who felt bad, left out, afraid, or hurt. So I decided to start each meeting with agreements that would make the activity as safe as possible. The agreement, called a "cooperative contract," promised that the participants and the leader would neither engage in nor allow any power play attempts to manipulate others or lies. It also required that participants would never do anything they did not honestly want to do and promised that the leader would not permit any transactions that came from the Critical Parent.

These contracts dramatically reduced the number of people who felt bad after these meetings. These calming, trust-enhancing agreements are a very important aspect of emotional literacy training today. They set the stage for the sometimes scary and difficult work that needs to be done to fully incorporate our feelings into our lives.

REFINED EXPERIENCE

The RAP center eventually dissolved, but the essence of "Stroke City" continued in emotional literacy training workshops. After twenty years of conducting these workshops, I have refined the techniques discovered in the sixties and developed new ones.

For instance, we found in my work with mental patients that paranoia generally builds itself around a grain of truth just as a pearl builds itself around a grain of sand. The standard psychiatric approach to paranoia was to disprove it point by point and to blame it on projection. So, for example, if David thinks that Maria hates him, traditional psychiatric wisdom presumes that it is David who hates Maria, and he is "projecting" his hatred onto her. This approach, in my opinion, made people more rather than less paranoid. Our approach, on the other hand was to find validation for David's paranoid feeling. We found that once the grain of truth in the paranoid fantasy was acknowledged, the person was usually able to let go of his paranoid ideas. So, if Maria admits that she is, in fact, angry at David's sloppiness, then David can let go of the idea that she hates him. That feeling, he can now realize, is a paranoid exaggeration of her actual feelings. David had simply picked up some negative feelings from Maria and blown them out of proportion. This method came from the work of R. D. Laing, the Scottish psychiatrist who pointed out that when we invalidate or deny people's experiences, or how they see things, we make mental invalids of them.

Ronald Laing found that when one's intuition is denied, one can be perfectly healthy yet be made to feel crazy. We tried to validate people's perceptions instead, giving them the chance to feel that their ideas were sane rather than demented. We found that our approach was an effective solution to people's problems with paranoid fears, while the standard psychiatric approach was, in fact, part of the problem and made it worse.

For instance, if Margaret's husband Chris was attracted to a neighbor, then Margaret may pick up subtle clues about his hidden infatuation. If she confronts Chris with her suspicions over and over again and he repeatedly denies them, her nagging intuitive fears might build to the point of paranoia.

Rather than accusing a person of being irrational and discounting their way of seeing things, finding the grain of truth in paranoid fantasy became a part of the training. By finding this truth, no matter how small, we could move a relationship away from paranoia and denial, back toward communication, feedback, and honesty. This is how I came to coin the now famous phase "Paranoia is heightened awareness."

EQ IN PRACTICE

These techniques and the others of emotional literacy training require honesty, trust, and the desire to change.

As I have developed these techniques over the years I have adopted them myself and invited my family members, friends, coworkers, and intimates to use them as well. I wrote books, delivered lectures, and held workshops. And all along, according to people around me, my emotional life improved. I began to give and take love and affection more freely, I got in touch with my feelings and the reasons for their existence, I learned to be honest about how I felt and decreased my tendencies to be defensive when confronted. Finally, I learned to acknowledge and sincerely apologize for my mistakes. Most important, however, is the realization that I am still a "work in progress," that I am still making improvements on my own Emotional Literacy.

One of the most frequent strokes I get from friends and trainees is that I practice what I teach and that my behavior is congruent with my theories. That is not to say that I have achieved perfect Emotional Literacy, only that I am making good progress and continue to learn day by day.

The chapters you are about to read contain a training program that is a proven method of developing emotional intelligence. I have seen it work for me and the people around me, so I know it can work for you.

WHAT IS EMOTIONAL LITERACY?

Your Emotional Literacy is made up of three abilities: the ability to understand your emotions, the ability to listen to others and empathize with their emotions, and the ability to express emotions productively.

To be emotionally literate is to be able to handle emotions in a way that improves your personal power and improves the quality of life around you. Emotional Literacy improves relationships, creates loving possibilities between people, makes cooperative work possible, and facilitates the feeling of community.

All of us have something to learn about our emotions. Some people grow up with a high level of emotional literacy, but I believe that few are as smart in the area of emotions as they should be. We all make emotional mistakes, and because of that, we can benefit from some form of Emotional Literacy training.

As a long-time teacher of Emotional Literacy, I have helped hundreds of people increase their emotional intelligence. I have seen the extreme discomfort most people, especially men, initially show at the mere mention of the word *emotions.* Men often fear that deep and painful secrets will be somehow unleashed if they reveal their feelings. Most often, people think that Emotional Literacy training will lead to a loss of control and power in their personal and business lives.

There is some validity to the fear that a loosening of our emotional restraints could get us into trouble. But Emotional Literacy is not a mere unleashing of the emotions. Just as important is learning to understand, manage and control them.

Emotions exist as an essential part of human nature. Without them, we would be psychopaths. By acknowledging and managing our feelings and listening to others in a productive way we will enhance rather than diminish our personal power.

Being emotionally intelligent means that you know what emotions you and others have, how strong they are, and what causes them. Being emotionally literate means that you know how to manage your emotions because you understand them. In emotional literacy training, you will learn how to express your feelings, when and where to express them, and how they affect others. You will also learn true empathy and learn to take responsibility for the way your emotions affect others.

Through this training, you will become an emotional gourmet, aware of the texture, flavor, and aftertaste of your emotions. You will learn how to let your rational skills work hand-in-hand with your emotional skills, adding to your ability to relate to other people. Hence, you will become better at everything you do with others: parenting, partnering, working, playing, teaching, and loving.

We should all take part in some form of emotional literacy training, because emotional mistakes are so common and destructive. If you don't think that is true, consider the following examples of emotional *illiteracy* I have gathered from the newspapers over the past year:

• When presented with a second-place award at a statewide competition, marching band leader Kent Baker of Virginia's Thomas Jefferson School, which consistently produces more National Merit Scholars than any school in the country, threw the award into a garbage can. The school's other director, Phil Simon, began to argue with the judges, saying his band deserved first place.

• Following a pee-wee football game in La Habra, an upper-middle-class community in California, an irate mother shouted obscenities at one of the referees and then grabbed him from behind as he tried to walk away. Three men then joined in the attack, punching him in the face and breaking his jaw, which had to be wired shut for several weeks.

• Warren Moon, the highly gifted quarterback of the Minnesota Vikings, was arrested and charged with spousal abuse after a frantic 911 call from the couple's children who alerted the police that "our daddy is beating our mommy."

• Top presidential adviser Dick Morris had to leave President Bill Clinton's campaign when it was reported that he shared state secrets with a prostitute in order to impress her.

• In England, a wealthy magistrate and his wife lied under oath, saying the wife had been driving their Range Rover when it ran into a wall. The couple, who had been drinking, were worried the magistrate might lose his driver's license and his seat on the bench. John Bosomworth, fifty, and his wife Anne, thirty-eight, were jailed for fifteen and nine months, respectively, when witnesses denied their story. And their marriage was wrecked by the stigma of being branded liars in their community.

Daily newspapers are filled with stories like these, accounts of successful and otherwise intelligent people making grave mistakes in emotionally charged situations. These are stories in which emotions like anger, fear, or shame makes smart people behave stupidly, rendering them powerless.

The truth is, we all make emotional mistakes, though perhaps not such extreme ones. Though our errors don't often find their way into the newspaper, almost all of us would have to admit that at one time or another we have been inordinately moved by anger, fear, insecurity, or jealousy, or have chosen not to take responsibility for an improper action. In the end these mistakes weaken us and our loved ones.

AN INTIMATE DINNER

I, of course, contend that Emotional Literacy increases personal power. I will make that point again and again throughout this book, but let me illustrate it here with a story. An event that began innocently enough as a simple dinner party of old friends rapidly escalated into a sexual encounter. Handled badly, it could have led to the ugly sort of incident that we read about so frequently in the newspapers.

Robert had been invited for dinner by Nancy and Jonathan, who'd been married to each other for some time. Nancy and Robert were old friends, going back to high school where they had dated briefly. Nancy had prepared a lovely meal and had even brought out candles for the event. When they sat down to eat, however, Robert did not seem to care about the décor or the food in front of him.

As he pushed his food around on the plate, Robert talked about his split with his wife. She had come home from work one evening and announced that she was leaving the relationship. She assured Robert that there was no other man, but gave no explanation for her departure. He was despondent and didn't know what would become of him.

"Face it, she just doesn't want me anymore," Robert blurted out miserably, after two glasses of wine. "Now how am I going to meet someone else? I'm not as good looking as I used to be, and I don't look forward to cruising the bars and answering personal ads."

Nancy understood perfectly what her old friend was talking about. The last year she had spent more and more time in the mirror scrutinizing her face for wrinkles, worrying that she looked old beyond her years. Aging had made her feel a new sense of insecurity. She had a little more wine.

Jonathan's day had been a tough one so he excused himself and went to bed. Shortly before midnight, Nancy and Robert found themselves alone.

The two old friends talked more about Robert's failed marriage. Conversation then turned to the romantic beginning and long duration of their wonderful friendship. Then Robert made a remark about his fading attractiveness. Nancy assured him that he was extremely handsome and should have no trouble at all finding another relationship. On the verge of tears, he squeezed Nancy's hand. She moved over on the couch and gave him a hug.

Then their cheeks and lips brushed, and they suddenly found themselves kissing each other.

"Stop," said Nancy. "We shouldn't do this."

Robert stood up, shaken. "I'd better leave," he said, too embarrassed to look at Nancy as he walked to the door. "I'm sorry." With one final glance at Nancy, he said good night and fled out the door.

LOSS OF COMMON SENSE

Nancy slept fitfully. The next morning, after lying awake and thinking for a long time, she told her husband what had happened. She explained that they had both been tipsy and depressed, and that Robert seemed so needy that she had lost her common sense, for a moment.

Jonathan's response was atypical. He was very upset at first, but then he remembered that they had once made a vow to be truthful with each other. He realized Nancy could have said nothing about the kiss and he probably would never have known. He imagined finding out in the worst possible way, a year from now, perhaps, when a guilty Robert confessed to Jonathan over a beer, or Nancy made a slip of the tongue.

Jonathan felt very secure about Nancy's love and he realized that Nancy was protecting him in a way by telling him about the incident. He could also see that she was both heartbroken about Robert's predicament and extremely worried that Jonathan would not forgive her. He also realized that Nancy had been feeling insecure about her looks and was vulnerable to Robert's attention.

Although his first feeling was anger, he realized that making a scene wouldn't make him feel better, or solve the problem. In fact, he would probably make a minor issue into a deep rift, damaging his marriage. Rather than exploding with anger or being overcome by jealousy, he tried to understand Nancy's actions from her point of view.

He told Nancy of his anger and jealousy, and having spoken about how he felt he was able to overcome these feelings. He put his arms around Nancy and hugged her warmly. Then, after explaining his intentions, he drove across town to Robert's apartment.

"Nancy told me what happened," he said as he sat down on the couch in Robert's living room. "I don't like it but I understand. I'm not angry. I assume that this was a mistake and won't happen again, right?"

"God no," Robert assured him. "I'm so sorry."

"Thanks then," said Jonathan, offering his hand in friendship. "I think things will be okay."

Stories like this generally end unhappily. Usually emotional mistakes of this sort remain a dark secret, undermining all the relationships involved. Sometimes, if the truth comes out, the result is a fight (verbal or physical) that leads to festering emotional wounds that often result in divorce.

It is the rare person who, like Jonathan, stops and thinks before deciding how to act on such an emotionally charged event. Yet Jonathan was able to speak about and sort out his feelings and keep them in check, until he could express them in a productive manner and prevent his life from careening out of control.

As a result of their emotionally literate exchange, Jonathan and Nancy found a deeper respect for each other and were able to open a dialogue about their relationship that actually strengthened their marriage. Talking about their emotions did not leave them feeling unprotected. Rather, it gave them a renewed sense of personal power and confidence about their relationship. It helped them flourish as a couple and enabled them to hold on to their friendship with Robert.

In many ways this story defines the very core of Emotional Literacy. Jonathan realized that he was angry and jealous. And he understood the reasons for those feelings. He also empathized with Nancy's affection for Robert and with her wish to comfort him. Jonathan could understand that she was flattered by Robert's passionate attention. In addition, he felt for Robert's sadness and fear of being alone. Once he understood his feelings better, Jonathan was able to control his impulse to lash out. Finally, Jonathan realized the importance of keeping the vows of complete honesty between him and Nancy.

All of this took skills that some people develop early in life, but that all of us can learn at any time. To devote time to learning these skills is to pursue Emotional Literacy.

THE FORGOTTEN HEART

Most people would not act the way Jonathan did in the above story. Why is that? Why do so many smart people act in emotionally stupid ways? Because we have lost touch with our feelings. Why has this happened? Because we have suffered and continue to suffer so many painful experiences that our emotional systems have shut down.

Why do our feelings shut down? Let me explain with an example of physical injury. Several years ago Chuck, a young grape farmer on the ranch next to mine in Mendocino County, absentmindedly reached into the rear of an operating hay baler. He felt a shock travel up his arm.

He pulled his hand back and looked at it. With an odd lack of emotion or alarm, he wondered where his index and middle finger had gone. Rotating his hand, he saw the two fingers hanging by threads of skin.

At first, he felt nothing. Then the pain came thundering in, and at last he realized the two fingers had been cut off. Today, after many operations, Chuck's fingers—reattached to his hand but lifeless—constantly remind him of his accident. He is able to speak about the accident calmly even though others cringe just thinking about it.

Why did Chuck at first feel nothing? Because his nervous system, to keep him from being overwhelmed, temporarily went into shock and blocked the pain. The shock reaction is highly useful. Because Chuck didn't feel the pain, he had time to absorb what had happened, to think rationally about it.

Numbing is a natural response to trauma. By temporarily sparing us the pain of a wound it gives us a chance to escape or to make lifesaving decisions we could not make if we were blinded by agony and horror. However, the physical numbness that follows physical hurt is limited. It is short-lived, providing just a minute or two of anesthesia before the pain comes flooding in.

The numbness that invades us as the result of emotional hurt is different. We have had psychological traumas so often that our minds fight them off by freezing up emotionally, by going numb. We survive psychological trauma by throwing up defense mechanisms—psychological walls—that insulate us and keep us from having disturbing thoughts, flashbacks, or nightmares. This may sound like a good thing, but it's a trade-off that can be very problematic. The psychological walls we erect to separate us from pain also separate us from our deepest feelings. What keeps us from feeling pain can keep us from feeling love or joy. In addition, these walls will on occasion collapse, and we will be flooded with chaotic, sometimes destructively strong, emotions.

To recover from emotional numbing we must be allowed to repeatedly recall the traumatic event and discuss it with a sympathetic listener. But typically we don't discuss or recover from such traumas. Instead, we just return to a state of numbness.

This happens for two reasons. One, emotional traumas such as parental abuse or alcoholism are often shrouded in secrecy and never "talked out." Two, such emotional injuries are usually not isolated, like Chuck's mishap, but are part of a long-term, destructive pattern. The emotional traumas of a lifetime are likely to linger and fester in the dark recesses of the soul, crippling the victim's emotional life for a lifetime.

My years of observation have persuaded me that the majority of us live in a state of semipermanent emotional shock continually reinforced by recurring painful experiences and have lost touch with most of our feelings. We forget traumatic incidents, don't remember how we felt, and don't know anyone who would listen patiently and sympathetically long enough to sort it all out. Consequently we go through life emotionally anesthetized, with most of our feelings locked up in our hearts, constantly disappointed in a wary and unreceptive world.

Certainly not all of us come from abusive homes or have alcoholic parents. But even the commonplace ups and downs of coming of age and going through our workaday lives without emotional outlet can still be quite painful and result in a certain degree of self-protective numbness.

Emotional shocks start early in childhood and continue throughout our lives. We are yelled at while playing an exciting game ("Will you shut up for a minute?"), or left alone when we are afraid. Our parents may fight or simply ignore each other. We are hit or mocked by other children, sometimes even by those we think are our friends.

One acquaintance of mine recalls how, when she was twelve, her two most beloved friends handed her a letter in which they made fun of the way she looked and the way she danced, told her they thought she was stupid and stuck-up, and announced that they were dropping her as a friend. To this day she is flooded by feelings of sadness and anger when she thinks about that awful experience.

Another friend relates how an older boy would come up to him every day while he waited in line for lunch in junior high school and make fun of his nose. This emotional torment went on for weeks.

Childhood is full of emotional stress and even abuse. Often the affection we crave is denied us or used to manipulate our behavior, given only if we are "good," withheld if we are "bad."

While all this is going on, we are silently urged—within our families and at school—to conceal what we feel and long for. To "spill our guts" about our feelings, we are taught, would be rude or indiscreet.

Our parents often care only about our most obvious problems—whether a bully is after us or whether we are having trouble making friends. They are not often interested in our subtler agonies—rebuffs, embarrassments, romantic disappointments or feelings of inadequacy. Some parents are uncomfortable asking their children how they feel and rarely discuss their own emotions.

HUNGER FOR EMOTIONS

As we adapt to all of these circumstances, we are forced to walk around with our thwarted passions and wounded feelings locked inside of us, not knowing what to do or who to speak to about them. We can't talk about our feelings, we don't understand them, and we understand the feelings of others even less. When in doubt, we hide our emotions or we lie about them or pretend not to feel them. We grow accustomed to operating without regard to, or even in spite of, our emotional selves.

Even in our love lives, where emotions are supposedly allowed free rein, many of us have been hurt so often that we remain subtly detached even in the throes of passionate love. Long-forgotten heartaches prevent us from fully letting go and giving ourselves to another without maintaining some secret, self-protective distance. We seldom allow ourselves the sweetest of emotional experiences—the vulnerable state of deeply loving someone without reservation.

Most of us sense that there should be more to life. We hunger for the intimacy of deep feeling. And we hunger for a connection to others, to understand someone and be understood by him or her. But how do we get there? We know in our hearts that being an emotional person, having strong passions—crying, rejoicing, even suffering—are rich, valuable experiences. In fact, we constantly seek indirect, artificial, or vicarious ways of experiencing emotions. We take drugs, fall in love with someone unattainable, or go to action, horror, and romantic movies; we watch sitcoms, melodramas, and soap operas on TV, searching for emotional stimulation. These activities afford us a taste of what we long for without the risks of real participation.

We all thirst for emotional stimulation, so much so that we will go to almost any lengths to get it. We gamble, jump off bridges with bungee cords attached to our ankles or parachute from airplanes. A far more dramatic and particularly horrifying example of this hunger for emotional experience is laid out by James Gilligan in his book, *Violence*. Gilligan has worked for many years with prison inmates guilty of savage murders. These men, he has found, invariably live in a state of extreme emotional numbness. They report having almost no feelings, emotional or physical, to the point of thinking of themselves as living dead.

They say they commit their unspeakably violent acts hoping that such excesses will break through their numbness and cause them to feel something. Such a person, having committed a brutal murder, may briefly feel that he has awakened from his deathlike anesthesia. But invariably the emotions stirred up by the crime subside and the numbness returns.

The numbness of these men doesn't come out of nowhere. Gilligan's research shows that in almost every case all these men were themselves victims of abuse, that they were battered by repeated physical and emotional traumas. This is a sobering example of how trauma leads to numbness and deep emotional pathology. Left unchecked, this pathology can be passed down through generations. Obviously, there's an urgent need to break the cycle of violence and emotional numbing. One way is by

21

learning emotional awareness, by developing empathy—the ability to feel what others are feeling. In deciding to sensitize ourselves to the emotions of others, we are making a definite moral choice, which will give us the capacity to be compassionate and kind.

EMPATHS AND PSYCHOPATHS

There are two kinds of people who seem destined to be powerful in the world: psychopaths, who feel nothing, or empaths, who are deeply in touch with the feelings of others.

Don't take these two types too seriously; they are caricatures and are extremely rare in real life. I bring them up to make a point.

Psychopaths can easily operate without the constraints that limit other mortals. They can lie, steal, extort, maim, and kill without guilt. When they get a hold over other people, they can become enormously powerful. Consider Caligula, the Roman emperor or Adolf Hitler. These are obvious examples, but examples can be found everywhere: in politics, business, gangs, even within certain families.

Empaths, on the other hand, gain power from their emotional skills. Born empaths have an innate gift for empathy that is fostered by their family and their teachers as they go through childhood and adolescence. Their talent for loving cooperation, for getting the best from people, gives them the power to counter the damage done by psychopaths.

Again, these are two extremes; many powerful people are neither full-blown psychopaths nor empaths. But if you observe them carefully, you will probably detect a preference toward one or the other style.

I, of course, am not encouraging you to work toward the empathic ideal.

EQ AND IQ

The value of being an emotional expert is not obvious to everyone, at least not as obvious as the value of being an intellectual expert. Research shows that if you have a high IQ (intelligence quotient)—it's more likely you will do well in school and become productive, successful, and a good earner. Not only that, you'll probably enjoy long life and good health.

It seems that such happy results come from intelligence alone, but they don't. In his groundbreaking best-seller, *Emotional Intelligence*, Daniel Goleman shows that emotional savvy is just as important in success as high IQ. Not only that, he shows that you need emotional intelligence to live a "good life"—one that allows you to enjoy the riches of the spirit. To live well, you need not only a high IQ but a high EQ (emotional quotient).

The term "EQ," though snappy, means less than you might think. It is a marketing concept, not a scientific term. An emotional quotient can't be measured and scored like an intelligence quotient. People have been rating IQ scientifically for nearly a century, though they argue about exactly what it means. Some say IQ precisely pegs an innate quality called intelligence. Others say it measures some less clear-cut quality of people who turn out to be successful in school, and eventually in life. Either way, you can validly and reliably measure a person's IQ, and it's proven a good thing to have a high one.

EQ on the other hand, can't be measured. Trying to rate somebody's EQ is like guessing how many beans there are in a quart jar: You can get a rough idea, but you can't figure it exactly. And you can't check yourself by counting, because emotions are a whole lot more elusive than beans.

Still, we can meaningfully speak of EQ as long as we don't claim to be able to measure it precisely. In chapter 2, there's a self-scoring questionnaire that will give you a rough idea of what your EQ might be, if it could be measured.

EMOTIONAL INTELLIGENCE AND EMOTIONAL LITERACY

The term "emotional intelligence" was coined by psychologists Peter Salovey and John Mayer. In his book *Emotional Intelligence*,

Daniel Goleman took an in-depth look at this powerful capacity and summarized the abundant research about it.

I coined the term "emotional literacy" eighteen years ago, and it first appeared in print in my book *Healing Alcoholism* in 1979. Since then, I have been working on a program that is designed to train people to develop emotional literacy skills.

Everyone has some emotional skills. Some people rank very high in this area, some rank low. Don't panic if you sense that you are among the latter. Training can help you move up the scale of emotional intelligence, which consists of five skills:

1. Knowing your own feelings: Do you know your true feelings? Many people can't define feelings of love, shame, or pride, nor can they tell the reason these undefined feelings are triggered. These same people often cannot even tell how strong their emotions are, even if asked to categorize them as subtle, strong, or overwhelming. If you can't gauge the strength of your feelings, you can't tell how much those feelings are affecting you and those around you.

2. Having a sense of empathy: Do you recognize other people's feelings? Do you understand why others feel the way they do? Do you identify with another's situation or motives? This is the ability to "feel for" other people, to feel their emotions as we do our own. When we are empathic, people's emotions resonate within us. We intuitively sense what those feelings are, how strong they are, and what caused them. This is difficult for some, but others do it so well that they can literally read a person's feelings like a book.

3. Learning to manage our emotions: Are you in control of your emotions? Knowing our emotions and those of others is not sufficient to become emotionally literate. We need to know when to express emotions and when to hold them back. We need to know when and how emotional expression or the lack of it affects other people. We need to learn how to assert our positive feelings, such as hope, love, and joy. And, we need to know how to let our negative emotions, such as anger, fear, or guilt, out in a harmless and productive way, and to postpone letting them out until a better time.

4. Repairing emotional damage: Do you know how to apologize and make amends? Being human, we all make emotional mistakes and hurt others. But we must learn to recognize what we have done wrong and fix it. To do this, we have to take responsibility, ask for forgiveness, and make amends. This can involve changing our behavior if it hurts someone. These tasks aren't easy, but if we don't carry them out, our unacknowledged mistakes will permanently poison our relationships.

5. Putting it all together: Once you have moved up the scale of Emotional Literacy, you develop a skill that I call "emotional interactivity." This means you can tune in to the feelings of people around you, sensing their emotional states and how to interact with them effectively.

Hannah used this ability to calm the waters at a Thanksgiving dinner which I attended a few years ago.

When Hannah and her husband arrived at the dinner party, she immediately noticed that there was some sort of trouble. Everyone—the couple giving the party, their three grown children, and four young grandchildren—seemed tense. Jim, one of the sons-in-law, was off in a corner nursing a drink. Other family members were laughing tensely. The host and hostess seemed sad and dazed.

Hannah took aside one of her friends and asked her why people seemed tense. She told her Jim had upset Judith, his wife's sister. Jim, a conservative thinker, had been arguing about child-rearing practices with Judith, who was much more liberal. The children had been horsing around and Jim, only half-jokingly, had told Judith she was spoiling her children and that they would turn into out-of-control teenagers, drug-addicted and sex-crazed. Judith got mad and told Jim in no uncertain terms to mind his own business. An uncomfortable feeling settled over the room.

Aunt Hannah saw that people looked to her to defuse the tension. She took Judith aside and let her vent her anger about Jim's unwanted criticism. Then she spoke privately with Jim and listened to him express his feelings about bratty children and indulgent parents. But Jim saw, after talking to Hannah, that his argument was ruining everyone's Thanksgiving. Hannah brought the two of them together with Mark, one of the husbands who liked them both. Jim, Judith, Mark and Hannah had a brief conversation in which hurt feelings were soothed and apologies were exchanged. By the time dinner was ready, everybody was ready to sit down and enjoy the meal.

Hannah had done the right amount of talking to the right people to restore a pleasant emotional climate. She encouraged Jim and Judith to get together with her over lunch and hash out their conflict further. She did all this easily and with a sense of loving good cheer.

How difficult is it to get to Hannah's level of emotional interactivity? Well, it's a whole lot easier if you do it while you are young as Daniel Goleman has shown in his book. It's just like learning to speak French or to play the violin; you can learn these skills far more easily in your youth, as you take advantage of a neurological "window of opportunity."

But if you didn't develop emotional skills during your youth, don't worry: you can still learn them as an adult. In fact, most people acquire some emotional literacy skills early in life and add to them later.

Even with average skills, and a little help from your friends, you can get by. But now that you have this book you have the chance to systematically improve your Emotional Literacy. All you have to do is study the lessons in these pages and put them into practice.

S U M M A R Y

What Is Emotional Literacy?

When we are emotionally literate we are able to handle difficult emotional situations that often lead to fighting, lying, lashing out and hurting other people.

We are under constant emotional trauma, most of it from simple everyday difficulties of living, some of it from betrayal and disappointment. Without an outlet all of this emotional pain makes us freeze up emotionally to protect ourselves. But by protecting ourselves within an emotional shell we lose touch with our feelings and become powerless to understand or control them.

We hunger for emotional experience and we seek it in many ways. Emotional literacy training is a direct and effective method of reestablishing contact with our feelings and their power, and thereby establishing good and loving relationships with others.

You can learn to to touch other people deeply with your emotions. You don't have to draw power from control and fear. Instead, you can be an empath, drawing power from love and sharing the power that love gives you.

You can train yourself to savor your own feelings and those of others. You can learn to understand and channel your emotions, listen and respond to others' needs, fix emotional damage, and navigate the world of feelings.

2

BECOMING AWARE OF YOUR EMOTIONS

Nearly everyone feels emotional distress when approached by a homeless beggar. Many of us immediately try to shut off our feelings, preferring to pretend that he doesn't exist or somehow deserves his fate. Others feel guilt, and may think that they should be giving more money to charity rather than buying luxury items like CDs or perhaps even this book. Still others will actually feel indignant and hostile toward this person, treating him as if he is an unwelcome intruder into their lives.

My own reaction varies. Sometimes I feel fearful or embarrassed, while at other times I feel guilty or angry. If I decide against helping, I look away and quicken my pace. If I decide to help I hand over some coins without looking the beggar in the eyes. If he says, "God bless you," I don't feel blessed. The situation brings me too many unpleasant thoughts about what it must be like to be destitute.

In the end I am happy to block the encounter from my mind. If I don't, I will feel off-balance and agitated for some time. Small wonder that I will go out of my way to avoid the homeless, even if it means crossing the street to do so.

This minute analysis of my emotional response may seem exaggerated and overdone, but think of your own experience. How much of what I describe goes through your mind when you run into a similar situation? How much of it do you experience without fully realizing your feelings? Most of us are not aware of the strong initial reaction that we quickly suppress in such situations.

Is there an emotional aftermath for you after these kinds of encounters? Do they leave you shaken or indifferent? Angry, guilty, or self-righteous? Do they bring thoughts of "heartless" Republicans, "tax-and-spend" Democrats, or welfare cheats?

Although we don't usually notice it, most of us go through such trying emotional events daily. Another driver cuts us off, a sales clerk is rude to us, a friend acts cold and distant. However, we are almost completely unaware of the complicated emotional nature in our everyday lives. Let us examine these emotional experiences in order to increase our awareness of them.

ROOTS OF EMOTIONAL AWARENESS

Emotions are inborn, generated automatically in the most primitive, reptilian, limbic portion of our brain. Fear, anger, sadness, love, and happiness serve as constant reminders of our animal nature. These emotions are changed and shaped by the experiences that surround us throughout our lives. If we are raised by abusive parents, for instance, research shows that we will most likely become abusive adults. Or, if we are raised by loving parents, we will be more likely to be loving adults.

Most of us have little awareness of how strong our emotions are or even what triggers them. In fact, few of us even know *what* emotions we feel. Without such awareness, we cannot hope to develop the empathic and interactive skills that are the highest achievement of Emotional Literacy. Developing awareness of our emotions is the subject of this chapter.

The purpose of the following questionnaire is to begin to

explore your emotional awareness. Although there is no sci-entifically valid EQ test, the questionnaire can give you a good idea of your level of emotional awareness, which is an essential part of emotional intelligence. As we saw in chapter 1, Emotional Literacy is the ability to understand our emotions as well as how to use them productively. Emotional awareness means:

- Knowing what we feel,

- Knowing what others feel,

- Finding out the cause of these feelings,

- Knowing the likely effect of our feelings on others.

EMOTIONAL AWARENESS QUESTIONNAIRE

Please answer these questions as honestly as possible. The point is not to look good, but to find out for yourself where you stand in terms of emotional awareness. If you can't decide whether your answer is Yes or No, answer Not Sure.

1.

A. I have noticed that sometimes when I find myself with a person who is very emotional I am surprisingly calm and without feeling.
Yes _____ No _____ Not Sure _____

B. At times when I am about to interact with people I don't know well, I feel sensations like heart palpitations, stomach cramps, a lump or dryness in the throat, or a shortness of

breath, but I don't know why this is happening.
Yes _____ No _____ Not Sure _____

C. Sometimes I am flooded by emotions that disorganize and confuse me.
Yes _____ No _____ Not Sure _____

D. From time to time, I am aware of having feelings of anger, from slight irritation to rage.
Yes _____ No _____ Not Sure _____

E. If another person is emotional, I am usually able to tell what emotion they feel, such as fear, happiness, sadness, hope, or anger.
Yes _____ No _____ Not Sure _____

F. I enjoy situations in which people are having strong positive emotions of love, hope, and joy, like at weddings or in church services.
Yes _____ No _____ Not Sure _____

2.

A. Sometimes after a difficult time with another person, I feel as if parts of my body are numb.
Yes _____ No _____ Not Sure _____

B. I take one or more over-the-counter drugs to deal with headaches, stomach and digestive symptoms, or body pains that my doctor can't explain.
Yes _____ No _____ Not Sure _____

C. I know I have very strong feelings, but I am frequently unable to talk about them with other people.
Yes _____ No _____ Not Sure _____

D. I am aware of having feelings of fear, from apprehension to terror.
Yes _____ No _____ Not Sure _____

E. Sometimes I can feel other people's feelings in my body.
Yes _____ No _____ Not Sure _____

F. I am appreciated by other people because I know how to cool down emotional situations.
Yes _____ No _____ Not Sure _____

3.

A. I can easily kill a small animal like a snake or chicken without feeling anything in particular.
Yes _____ No _____ Not Sure _____

B. I am ofter jumpy and irritable, and I can't help it.
Yes _____ No _____ Not Sure _____

C. I find myself lying about my feelings because I am embarrassed to speak about them.
Yes _____ No _____ Not Sure _____

D. I am aware of having strong feelings of love and joy.
Yes _____ No _____ Not Sure _____

E. I often do things for other people because I sympathize with them and can't say "no" to people.
Yes _____ No _____ Not Sure _____

F. I am good at helping people sort out their emotions because I usually understand why they are feeling them.
Yes _____ No _____ Not Sure _____

4.

A. I can be around people who are suffering physical pain without getting upset about it.
Yes _____ No _____ Not Sure _____

B. I get sweaty palms around people I don't know.
Yes _____ No _____ Not Sure _____

C. I know I have strong feelings, but most of the time I don't know what those feelings are.
Yes _____ No _____ Not Sure _____

D. I am pretty good at knowing what I feel and why.
Yes _____ No _____ Not Sure _____

E. Sometimes other people's feelings are very clear to me, and that can be a problem.
Yes _____ No _____ Not Sure _____

F. I can usually handle people who have strong feelings and unload them on me.
Yes _____ No _____ Not Sure _____

5.

A. I am almost always a rational person and have no problems with my emotions.
Yes _____ No _____ Not Sure _____

B. I have been in love and suddenly, inexplicably lost that feeling completely.
Yes _____ No _____ Not Sure _____

C. I am overwhelmed by bad mood sometimes.
Yes _____ No _____ Not Sure _____

D. When I have to make an important desision, I usually know how I feel about it, whether it be scared, excited, angry, or some other combination of emotions.
Yes ＿＿ No ＿＿ Not Sure ＿＿

E. In a competitive situation in which I am winning or clearly superior, I feel bad for the other person.
Yes ＿＿ No ＿＿ Not Sure ＿＿

F. When I am in a room full of people, I can tell how the group is feeling—excited, angry, bored, or scared.
Yes ＿＿ No ＿＿ Not Sure ＿＿

6.

A. I very, very rarely cry.
Yes ＿＿ No ＿＿ Not Sure ＿＿

B. Sometimes when I watch a TV commercial, tears come to my eyes, and I don't really understand why.
Yes ＿＿ No ＿＿ Not Sure ＿＿

C. Sometimes when I am feeling bad, I can't tell if I am scared or angry.
Yes ＿＿ No ＿＿ Not Sure ＿＿

D. I am a person who at times feels shame and guilt.
Yes ＿＿ No ＿＿ Not Sure ＿＿

E. I have had the opportunity to shoot an animal like a bird, rabbit, or deer, and was not able to do it because I felt bad for the animal.
Yes ＿＿ No ＿＿ Not Sure ＿＿

F. I often change the way I act toward another person because I figure it will make things easier between us.
Yes _____ No _____ Not Sure _____

Now that you have answered all the quesstions, you can score the questionnaire. Count up the number of "Yes" responses on all questions marked A. Write that number (from 1 to 6) in the space marked "A" below. Repeat that process with B, C, D, E, and F questions.

A. _____
B. _____
C. _____
D. _____
E. _____
F. _____

There now should be a number (from 1 to 6) next to each letter above. You can use these numbers to create a bar chart and determine your emotional awareness profile.

Create a blank bar chart similar to the one below on a separate piece of paper and fill in the boxes based on your scores. For example, if you answered "Yes" to six D questions, fill in the D column all the way up through the number 6 row. If you answered "Yes" to two B questions, fill in the B column through the number 2 row. Shade your remaining scores. When you have finished, you will have a bar chart similar to the example below:

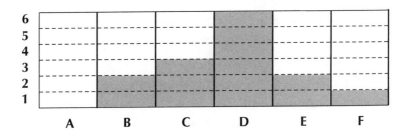

This profile is based on a scale that ranges from low to high emotional awareness. I developed the scale to illustrate the levels of emotional awareness that people experience.

THE EMOTIONAL AWARENESS SCALE

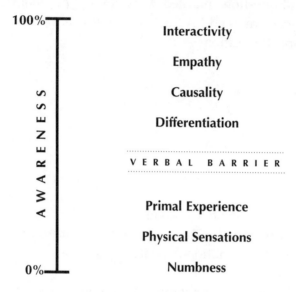

What follows is an explanation for each level of the emotional awareness scale. Learning about these levels will help you interpret and understand the questionnaire scores and personal profile you have just completed for yourself, which we will come back to at the end of the chapter.

Numbness. People in this state are not aware of anything they call feelings or emotions. This is true even if they are under the influence of strong emotions. Strangely, other people are usually more aware of the numb person's feelings than she is. While a person in this state may not feel her own emotions, those around her can perceive them from cues such as facial expression, blushing, and tone of voice; however, she is likely to report only coldness or numbness when asked how she feels.

36

Her emotions are in a sort of deep freeze, unavailable to awareness.

For example, Lucas was a successful thirty-eight-year-old accountant, whom I met, with his wife Clara, during a mediation of their marital difficulties. Clara had just given a tight-lipped, tearful account of her anger and hurt about the way things were between them. I turned to Lucas. He looked stiff and uncomfortable.

"How do you feel, Lucas?"

"Well, I feel that she is being unfair."

"Okay. We can talk about that later, when we get to your point of view. How does the way she talks about you make you feel, emotionally?"

He hesitates, wriggles in his chair, thinks. Finally, looking embarrassed, he adds: "I guess I don't feel anything."

"I wonder . . . Let's see, do you have any sensations in your body? Some people feel butterflies in their stomach, lumps in their throat, a painful tingling feeling, or dizziness. . . ."

"Well, I feel sort of numb all over. Not now so much but when she was talking."

"You don't feel anything?"

"Not really. In fact, I feel really distant, as if I were in a fog."

For someone like Lucas, this state of unawareness is a common experience. On occasion, however, his anger breaks through. This usually happens under the influence of alcohol or other drugs, and is vented in a sharp, brief outburst. A few times a year Lucas goes on a drinking spree. When that happens he becomes nasty, emotionally abusive, and on occasion breaks some furniture. Then he sobers up, goes through a period of guilt and self-abuse, and soon becomes a detached, hard-working accountant again. These outbursts leave him feeling shaken and guilty, but he is too bewildered by his own emotions to arrive at any insight. Eventually renewed numbness returns.

In psychiatric terms, this state of emotional numbing is known as *alexithymia*.

Physical Sensations. At this level of emotional awareness, the physical sensations that accompany emotions are experienced but not the emotions themselves. In psychiatric terms, this is called *somatization*.

A person might feel his quickened heartbeat but is not aware that he is afraid. She may notice a pressure in her chest but does not identify it as depression. He might experience a hot flash, a chill, a knot in his stomach, or ringing in his ears, tingling sensations, even shooting pains. She may feel all of these *sensations* of the emotion, but not be aware of the emotion itself.

These sensations are never very far from awareness, even for a person who is emotionally detached. Lucas, for instance, is conscious of physical sensations when he is questioned, even though he does not associate them with any particular emotions.

As Lucas describes his numb state, I pursue my questioning:

"Good, that is a clear description of what happens to you emotionally when your wife complains about you. But let's look into your reaction further. Do you have any of the other physical sensations I described before? What else is going on?"

"Actually, I also feel a tight band around my forehead."

"Anything else?" I scrutinize his face. "Do you feel a headache?"

"Not really, but I have a strange feeling that I'm going to get one. I get pretty bad headaches. I'm going to have to take some double-strength painkillers when we leave here."

When people live in this state of emotional illiteracy, they often consume drugs that target physical sensations with an emotional origin. Although these drugs can have detrimental side effects, they work temporarily for the person who is trying to cope with his emotional conflicts. They do this by eliminating headaches, stomachaches, and other physical sensations that would remind them that there are some emotional problems that need attention.

Consequently, the conflicts don't go away, and the emotional issues remain unresolved. The drugs may temporarily erase or improve the unpleasant sensations, but they throw the body's chemistry out of balance and lead to harmful short- and long-term effects.

Lucas, as an example, takes large amounts of over-the-counter painkillers for his sore back and headaches. His doctor has warned him that ibuprofen and acetaminophen taken with alcohol can cause liver damage, so he takes aspirin, which gives him an upset stomach for which he takes Maalox. He drinks two cups of strong coffee in the morning to wake up, then drinks diet cola all day to keep himself alert. He also smokes to deal with tension and anxiety. At night he likes to have "a glass or two" of wine to help him unwind and get to sleep. None of this self-medication leaves him feeling very good, but at least it makes his discomfort manageable.

When people take large quantities of drugs and/or alcohol regularly, they can no longer accurately interpret their bodily experiences. Are these experiences emotional or chemical, exaggerated or understated, healthy or diseased? When a person is so frequently and heavily self-medicated, it is very difficult to tell.

While in this state of emotional unawareness, people are able to inflict great emotional damage on others. Strong emotions that are unacknowledged can cause irrational behavior and pain and numbness. But irrational behavior perpetuates the cycle. People act out, feel extreme guilt, then shut down, narrowing their emotional awareness and creating a familiar cycle of abuse, numbness and emotional illiteracy.

Primal Experience. In the primal stage, a person is conscious of emotions, but they are experienced as a heightened level of disturbing energy that is not understood and cannot be put into words. Consequently, a person in this emotional state is very vulnerable and responsive to emotions but unable to comprehend or control them. A person in the primal experience stage is more likely to have uncontrolled emotional outbursts and fits of impulsiveness or depression than the person whose emotions are frozen out of awareness. The person in the primal stage will

39

usually be the one to fall apart first when stress bears down on a whole group.

Lucas, as an example of the opposite, works in an extremely high-pressure and stressful environment. At tax time, he is acknowledged as a "cool head" and trusted with crucial decision making. His coworkers and even his supervisors do not find his coldness particularly likable, but he is highly valued by his employers for his efficiency.

Because of this paradox, some people conclude that emotional awareness and responsiveness are handicaps. However in the long run, achieving high emotional literacy skills and awareness of emotional information will lead to personal effectiveness and power even in our emotionally illiterate world. This is because a highly emotionally literate person will know how to control her feelings when necessary. This may not be possible in situations where extreme ruthlessness and emotional coldness are required but these types of situations will be avoided by the emotionally literate person in any case. There are some jobs, like contract killer or executive in charge of downsizing, in which a high level of emotional awareness makes it impossible to perform effectively.

The Verbal Barrier. Crossing this linguistic barrier requires an environment that is friendly to emotional information. Once it has been crossed, however, a person is able to talk about his emotions in such a way that he develops an increasing awareness of his feelings.

Lately, learning to speak about our emotions is becoming even more difficult because many people spend their working days in intimate contact with machines like computers instead of people.

And people's contact with machines does not end at work. At home people attach themselves to their television, video games, stereo, or computer, all of which are isolating.

People who spend so much time in isolation are not likely to analyze their own emotions and lose interest in emotions all together. It is a sad fact that many people wait for the TV commercials to transact their emotional business, if they conduct any such business at all. Many people do not pay attention to emotional conflicts until their friendships are wrecked, their marriages are near divorce or their relationships with their children are badly damaged.

After all, isn't it easier to sit down and watch television than to carry on a meaningful discussion with a member of your family? Few realize how such a choice can insulate people from their own emotions and those of others. Without analyzing our feelings we can never hope to escape from a state of numbness, physical turmoil, or emotional chaos. And we can never hope to have fulfilling relationships with others.

We need an environment that welcomes and encourages emotional discourse, where we can share our emotions honestly with people who will honestly share theirs. Finding such an environment is essential to the development of emotional awareness. Even a community of two will do to start.

Differentiation. This level of awareness reflects a step toward recognizing different emotions and their intensity as well as learning how to speak about them to others. At this stage we become aware of the differences between basic emotions like anger, love, shame, joy, or hatred. We also realize that any feeling can occur at various intensities. Fear can go from apprehension to terror. Anger can range from irritation to hatred. Love can be felt at many levels from affection to passion.

As we cross the verbal barrier (a virtual wall for some), we begin to recognize that we often have several feelings at once. Some of these feelings are strong and obvious, while others are weak and hidden. Some are brief while others are long-lasting.

For example, when we are feeling overwhelmed by jealousy, we may realize that the main feeling is anger combined with weaker feelings of unrequited love, tinged by shame. Someone else might experience jealousy as feelings of fear combined with intense hate.

Let's continue to pursue our troubled accountant, Lucas. When I asked him why he responded so strongly to his

41

wife's recriminations, he said, "Because I was a little annoyed, I suppose."

"How about sad?"

"I guess so. . . . Yeah, sad too," he said with emphasis, "and afraid that I'll lose control and retaliate and hurt her feelings. She is so thin-skinned."

"How angry do you feel?" I asked again.

"Not very angry, just annoyed."

"But if you are not that angry, why would you lose control?"

"I suppose I am angry." He was quiet for a moment, during which I noticed his color redden. "Yeah, I guess I am."

"Furious?"

There was a long silence. By now Lucas's face was very red. Turning to his wife, his voice full of guilt and apprehension, Lucas finally said, "Yeah, thinking it over, I would say that I do feel very strongly about it."

I questioned Lucas further, making sure that I was not putting words in his mouth. As I helped him become aware of his true feelings, it turned out that Lucas felt intense, blinding anger about his wife's accusations and was extremely afraid of "losing it" and "blowing up at her." And when he thought about it, he also felt despondent and afraid. Quite a bit going on for someone who initially claimed to feel nothing.

Causality. As we begin to understand the exact nature of our feelings, we also begin to understand the causes of those feelings, the event that triggered our emotional response, and why we feel strong pride or hate, whence our fear.

To illustrate, Peter began feeling jealous the night he noticed his girlfriend Jennifer laughing at their friend Michael's jokes. At first he was unwilling to admit feeling jealous, even to himself, because he prided himself on feeling confident and secure. But he caught himself being irritable with Jennifer and had to admit that he was probably jealous.

Here the inevitability of emotional interconnections between people has to be understood. In spite of claims to the contrary, we can cause feelings in others and they can cause feelings in us. In this case, Jennifer's apparent flirtation with Michael made Peter jealous.

We begin to discover the alchemy of emotions; how our emotional tendencies (to be thin-skinned, assertive, or jealous) combine with the emotional tendencies and behavior of others.

Eventually we are able to investigate, and in most cases understand, why we feel what we feel. Peter, feeling embarrassed, explained his jealousy to Jennifer. She told him she never meant to make him feel that way, but that after a hard week she enjoyed a good laugh. Now that she was aware of Peter's feelings of jealousy, she decided to make an effort to pay more attention to Peter while Michael entertained them.

Empathy. As we learn the different emotions that we feel, the various intensities with which we feel them, and the reasons for them, and as our awareness of our own emotions becomes textured and subtle, we begin to perceive and intuit similar texture and subtlety in the emotions of those around us.

Empathy is a form of intuition about emotions. The workings of empathy are quite amazing to the novice, because they seem to depend on an ability that, at times, feels dangerously like clairvoyance.

When being empathic we don't figure out or think about, see, or hear other people's emotions. It has been suggested that empathy is actually a sixth sense with which we perceive emotional energies in the same manner in which the eye perceives light. If that is the case, then empathy takes place on an intuitive channel—separate from the other five senses—that goes directly to our awareness. Emotional illiteracy occurs when we fail, in our formative years, to develop that sixth sense. Usually we learn to suppress it because of the constant lying about and discounting of feelings that are commonplace to childhood experiences. Some people are born "empaths" with high sensitivity to emotions, and others are emotionally tone deaf. Most of us are somewhere in the middle, and all of us can learn or relearn empathic awareness.

Empathy, like all intuition, is imprecise and of little value until we develop ways of objectively confirming the accuracy of our perceptions.

For example, returning to Peter and Jennifer's situation, Jennifer had begun to suspect that Peter was becoming more and more uncomfortable around Michael. Her intuition told her, even though he denied it at first, that he felt jealous. She couldn't understand why he would feel this way, since she was extremely affectionate and attentive toward him during their private time together. She thought that Peter's jealousy might have to do with Michael's good looks, and began to wonder if Peter was insecure about his appearance.

Jennifer had been reading an article about Emotional Literacy and learning some of the techniques, which she had described to Peter.

When Jennifer decided to ask Peter if he was feeling jealous, Peter's first impulse was to deny it. He thought his jealousy was childish and was embarrassed to admit to it.

"Be honest, please" asked Jennifer, reassuring him she wouldn't think less of him.

"All right, I do feel a little jealous," he admitted at last.

"But Michael isn't especially attractive to me. I'm much more attracted to you."

"No, that's not it. You've made it pretty clear how much you like me," he said smiling sheepishly. "But you know how tongue-tied I get sometimes. Michael is so at ease and funny, aren't you kind of attracted to that?"

Jennifer thought a moment. "Well, I guess so. But you're just as funny in your own way, when we're alone. It's fun hanging out with someone like him, but you're the person I want to be in a relationship with. There are always going to be other people we both know who have qualities we like, but I'm with you because you have the qualities that are most important to me; because I love you." She gave him a hug and they embraced happily for a moment. But now there was something Peter needed to clear up.

"Can I ask you a question about this?" Jennifer agreed eagerly. "I feel like you keep your distance from me when he's around. Actually, I am afraid you lose interest in me when the three of us get together."

She was shocked. "Not at all!" But thinking it over she realized why he might feel that way. "I guess I've always thought it's rude to be affectionate with a partner in front of someone who's single."

"I can see that." Peter nodded thoughtfully.

"But maybe I've gone too far. I think we could hold hands sometimes or sit closer together without making Michael feel bad. I'll try to do that more. I just really want your friends to like me and I was being very careful to be considerate."

Peter's intuition that Jennifer was attracted to something about Michael was confirmed. Also confirmed was that she was avoiding contact with Peter when the three were together. But his fear that she was romantically interested in Michael, or that Michael had eclipsed him, turned out to be untrue. Instead, he was pleased to learn how much she wanted to fit in with his friends, and how hard she tried to be considerate of other people's feelings.

His intuition was validated, his fears allayed, and he discovered something new about Jennifer—her thoughtfulness—which he found very lovable.

Peter had sometimes dismissed Jennifer's declarations of love as exaggerations, but hearing her talk calmly about why she'd chosen to be with him, he suddenly felt more sure of her love. Just a few of the many fruits of an emotionally literate dialogue.

By following up her hunch about Peter's jealousy, and by initiating a discussion with him, Jennifer was forging a stronger, more emotionally literate connection between herself and Peter. Her intuition proved correct, and that gave her a chance to change in a way that helped Peter feel better. We hone our powers of empathy by asking questions; if the other person is unwilling to be honest and supply truthful feedback we cannot progress. Honest feedback is the sole means of heightening one's empathic intuitions.

This process of honest discussion and gathering feedback greatly improves the accuracy of our subsequent empathic perceptions. We learn to become aware of the intensity of other people's feelings and to understand why they occur, sometimes as clearly as we do our own. Eventually as our Emotional Literacy improves, our empathic perceptions become more accurate and reliable. We learn to trust our feelings and perceptions, and to be more open about them. This transformation is achieved through formulating continual perceptions, gathering feedback, and correcting our misinterpretations.

It is important here to draw a distinction between empathy and sympathy. Sympathy is an intellectual process with which we can visualize another person's emotional state and that helps us understand and even predict how he or she might feel and act. However, sympathy is not an emotional but a mental process that stands in relation to empathy as a paint-by-the-numbers canvas stands to an artist's rendering. We can fill in the proper spaces with the rights colors or emotions and we will get a reasonable facsimile of the real thing without being emotionally involved in the process. Empathy is quite different—it involves our own emotions so that we understand what others feel because we feel it in our hearts as well as visualize it in our minds.

Sympathy is a poor substitute for empathy but it is not uncommon for people to be unable to empathize with certain emotions in other people. In that case, sympathy is clearly better than nothing at all. But to progress to the next level of emotional awareness true empathy is required.

Interactivity. Being "merely" an empathic person—an "empath" if you will—has its disadvantages. The empath is keenly aware of a complex universe of emotional information not largely perceived by others, some of it painful, perhaps even unbearably so.

Knowing how others feel does not necessarily mean we know what to do about it. People's emotional behavior seems to call for a response but a response may not be wanted, welcome, or possible. Being highly empathic in a largely emotionally illiterate world can literally drive a person mad. An empathic person needs to know what to do with his awareness. Emotional interactivity requires knowing how people will respond to each other's emotions and when that interaction might escalate for better or for worse. It means knowing people's emotions well enough to know how one person will react to anger or fear or sadness or how another person will respond to sexuality, joy, or optimism.

Emotional interactivity is based on the most sophisticated level of awareness, the ability to realize what you are feeling and what others are feeling, and to anticipate how emotions will interact. This further enables you to anticipate how two different people, given their usual emotional proclivities, will react in a given situation.

Emotions merge, fade, grow, and shrink in each other's presence and over time.

Interactive awareness has to do with understanding the way emotions, like chemicals, combine to create new substances that one could not have guessed at from examining the component parts. These combinations can be creative, inert, or explosive, as in the chemist's laboratory. The ability to predict these reactions can come only from a great deal of accumulated experience or wisdom.

The complicated awareness of how emotions combine with each other, within people, and between people is the highest level of emotional sophistication.

While this sounds very complicated, a simple example of this wisdom at work is the way my friend David introduced his new girlfriend to his teenage daughter, Robyn, who tended to be shy and retiring.

Knowing that a face-to-face meeting over dinner might be hard for Robyn, David instead decided that his new girlfriend should come along while he drove his daughter to another city to visit her mother. This gave Robyn a chance to observe him with his new partner while she sat in the backseat, safely out of sight.

This way Robyn learned about her stepmother-to-be and had more of a chance to get to know and like her than she might at a potentially difficult dinner, where she might be nervous about being in the limelight.

David's sense that the first option was not very good arose from his heightened awareness of emotional interactions.

Another more complicated example is John and Deidre, a couple who had been in a month-long conflict. John was angry because Deirdre was spending more and more time at her new job, which was the first job she had ever had that really excited and fully challenged her. John was used to being the principal wage earner and was feeling inexplicable jealousy and envy. He had always been prone to emotional outbursts, and lately he felt dangerously close to losing his temper.

John and Deirdre had a good relationship of many years, and John knew that Deirdre loved and trusted him. However, she was easily frightened by displays of anger.

They had had a number of unproductive emotionally charged conversations, and Deirdre was beginning to retreat emotionally from him. John was feeling increasingly at a loss.

Brooding about what to do, John remembered the time he and Deirdre had had a heated disagreement over dinner with her sister Marsha. Marsha's presence helped John control his temper, and Marsha had acted as a calm advocate for Deirdre, which seemed to embolden Deirdre to hold her own in the debate.

John decided that it would be a good idea to invite Marsha over for Sunday brunch, explaining that he wanted her help to discuss Deirdre's work. He talked the idea over with Marsha and with her approval called Deirdre. Marsha, Deirdre and John agreed on a good time and after a pleasant meal John suggested that Marsha sit near Deirdre while he told her how he had been feeling.

John knew that if he let his feelings loose under less protected circumstances he might get angry and Deirdre would feel overpowered. He might get her to cut back on her work, but not without creating serious emotional repercussions later.

Marsha was a good choice for a mediator because she liked both of them and was not scared of John. Her self-assured, calming influence gave John the confidence to speak out clearly and gave Deirdre the strength to stand up to his demands without being intimidated.

On the other hand, if Deirdre was a different person and John knew that she would not be afraid to hear him out even if he yelled, the situation would be very different and would call for a different, perhaps more direct approach, that would not require bringing in Deirdre's sister to mediate.

John was aware of his own feelings and tendencies and equally aware of Deirdre's. He knew from experience how their different styles were likely to interact, namely, that he would shout, and she would likely comply but later be unhappy and irritable. He took steps to prevent the problems that would result if he acted impulsively. This kind of deliberate analysis of the emotional landscape of a relationship is the hallmark of emotionally literate interactivity.

Interactivity is a much-used concept in the communication age. In that context, it refers to intelligent interaction instead of passive acceptance. The same is true of emotional interactivity. Interactive awareness enables us to register the emotions within and around us, and to begin to see how they can be molded to creative ends, instead of going unnoticed and being allowed to run out of control. We can use our emotional awareness to have easier, more positive and productive interactions.

Interactivity empowers empaths to use their awareness to navigate powerful emotional situations in a skillful way. Thus interactivity is the link between emotional *awareness*, which is the subject of this chapter, and Emotional *Literacy*, the subject of this book.

YOUR EMOTIONAL AWARENESS PROFILE

Let's get back to the bar chart that you generated with the questionnaire on pages 30–35. First of all, I want to reemphasize that this profile is not a measurement of Emotional Literacy but an examination of awareness, which is an important aspect of Emotional Literacy. The A questions test for emotional numbness (EN); B questions test for physical symptoms (PS); C questions refer to chaotic primal experience (CE); D questions test for differentiation (DF); E questions for empathy (EM); and F for interactivity (IA). The profile you generated will help you see what kind of work you need to do to improve your Emotional Literacy. The three most common profiles are:

Low awareness profile:

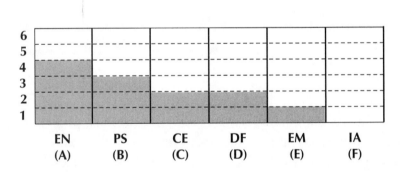

If your profile looks like this you are a person who hasn't paid much attention to your feelings and tends to be puzzled by the feelings of others. Most of the time you are unaware of feeling any emotions at all; they're not part of your normal life as far as you can tell. On the occasions that you have a very strong emotional response, you feel anger or fear and you do everything you can to overcome that unwelcome state. You need to work on your Emotional Literacy.

High awareness profile:

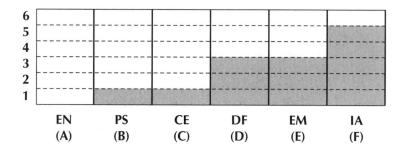

If your profile looks like this, your emotions are part of your everyday life awareness. You know how you feel, why, and how strongly most of the time. You feel comfortable talking about emotional subjects and understand other people's emotions, but you may find that your awareness is a problem. If you talk about your emotions you may create problems for yourself, and if you don't you may feel like a stranger in a strange land where no one sees what you see. You are in a very good position to develop a high level of Emotional Literacy.

The average awareness profile:

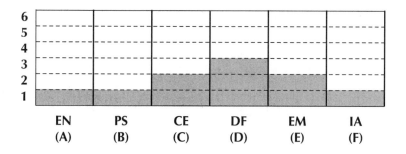

If your profile looks like this, you are aware of your feelings but don't always know what to do about them. You understand some of your emotions but are puzzled by others. You are able to empathize at times but at times you are left cold by other people's feelings. Most of the time when in an emotional state your feelings are a bothersome, chaotic jumble which you try to get away from by ignoring them. When you try to talk about them to other people the results are mixed. Sometimes feelings are resolved, sometimes they are made worse. You are the person most likely to profit from this book.

BEYOND AWARENESS

Awareness is an essential aspect of personal power, but, as we have seen, it is not sufficient by itself to produce the changes that Emotional Literacy requires. As a person's emotional awareness expands he is able to learn the additional skills necessary to act in an increasingly emotionally literate way. Learning awareness and literacy are the essential lessons of chapters 3 to 8.

S U M M A R Y

The Emotional Awareness Scale

Awareness is an essential part of Emotional Literacy. You can question yourself on an emotional awareness scale and see where you stand.

The scale, from lowest to highest awareness, is as follows:

Numbness: You haven't any awareness of your feelings.

Physical sensations: Your emotions register physically (for instance, as headaches or dizziness) but you still aren't aware of the emotions themselves.

Primal experience: You're conscious of emotions but you don't know what they are. You can't discuss them or understand them.

Differentiation: By crossing the verbal barrier and talking about your feelings you learn to differentiate between anger, love, shame, joy, or hatred.

Causality: You can not only tell emotions apart, you can also see what causes them.

Empathy: You are aware of other people's emotions.

Interactivity: You are sensitive to the ebb and flow of emotions around you and how they interact.

Knowing your emotions, being aware of them in yourself and others, is the first step to becoming Emotionally Literate.

3

TRAINING TO BE
EMOTIONALLY LITERATE

You don't have to live in a state of emotional numbness, nor are you doomed to go through life feeling dejected, irritable, anxious, tortured by impulses or out of control. And if you are an openly responsive empath, you don't need to be enslaved by other people's feelings. With a supportive environment and a cutting-edge technique, you can turn your emotions into a source of joy.

Research shows you can heal even extreme trauma in an environment that lets you express strong feelings. In an emotionally literate environment you can go right to the heart of your problem and slowly but surely deal with it. The feelings that result from emotional trauma, including flashbacks, nightmares, anxiety attacks, and depression will lessen in time or even vanish when discussed with sympathetic friends, family, counselors, or therapy group members.

Not only that, you will find a new emotional self and your relationships with others will be transformed.

It might seem that pursuing your emotional self is a foolhardy adventure in a world such as ours. Those people around you who keep their strong feelings out of sight seem to have an advantage—they can stay the course when others are swamped by feelings. But in the long run, a truly productive life requires that we include emotional information in our choices. From a routine discussion of the news over breakfast to a critical decision such as choosing whom to marry, you vitally need emotional knowledge for a well-rounded, effective approach to life.

Few things are as exciting as the rediscovery or refinement of our emotional selves. It is this excitement that fuels people's interest in emotional literacy workshops and training.

THE APPEAL OF AN EMOTIONALLY LITERATE LIFE

I have found that when people glimpse the implications of an emotionally literate life, they are often struck by its potential beauty. This drives some people to become emotional warriors in a crusade against emotional illiteracy.

A recently widowed grandmother of 55 who took one of my workshops in Germany wrote me as follows:

Since I was a child I have known that life can be lived differently and I always had the vague idea that it had to do with honesty about feelings and no compromise about what I want, together with a strong love of people. I have tried to love people, I love my daughters and my grandchildren, but I see now that love is not enough. It can go very wrong, as in my marriage. From now on I will be a crusader for emotional honesty. Nothing less will do. Thanks for showing me the way.

This woman has set her goal very high, but with determination and courage, she can reach it. So can you. Not all at once, but over time. The key is to work systematically. At the end of this chapter I briefly describe the three training stages I have developed to help you reach your own goal of Emotional Literacy: opening the heart, surveying the emotional landscape, and taking responsibility.

THE TRAINING PROCESS

But first, let's take a look at the process that this training follows.

Over the years I have found we can open a gateway through our emotional barriers by expressing our loving nature. Emotional literacy learning begins and ends with the heart.

In my work with couples in difficulty, women often complain that the man does not love them or doesn't love them enough, that he does not express his loving feelings, or that he gladly takes affection but doesn't give it.

To be sure, there are always a few men who simply don't love their wives (or partners). But more often the men *do* love them but suffer from an inability to express their love convincingly. These men often wonder, eventually, why it is that they can't be more loving. This disability to show love is one example of emotional numbness.

Women make this complaint often about men, but men can have the same grievance about women—that they are cold and don't show affection. Emotional numbness is by no means exclusive to men. But no matter which sex is involved, the solution is the same: Loosen the fetters upon your heart.

Let me give an example: Jack and Gina came to my office and were very upset. After a year and a half of blissful marriage, things were falling apart. They were fighting about "everything," and their fights were getting so bad that their relationship seemed destined to end in disaster.

In a very brief preliminary discussion I could tell that they were still in love, but were just unable to deal with the emotional issues that were piling up between them. I could have spent quite a bit of time with questions about their childhood or by trying to mediate their arguments, but instead I suggested that they start talking about the good things in each other that made them fall in love in the first place.

This calmed them down and got them back onto common ground. Soon they were speaking civilly to each other and seemed happy as they remembered the "good old days" of their relationship. In essence, they had reopened their hearts to each other.

Over the next month, I had them explore their emotional makeup. Using techniques of emotional literacy training, I asked them to talk about their feelings for each other, revealing their anger, their deepest fears, and their greatest hopes. By the time they finished surveying each other's emotional landscape, they had a new understanding and appreciation for one another.

With this new understanding they were now in a position to recognize how they had damaged their relationship with a series of hurtful missteps that needed to be corrected.

Now they were ready to accept responsibility for their actions. Painfully they admitted their wrongdoings and accepted each other's apologies. This was difficult but brought them great relief, often mixed with tears of joy and hope. Their mutual love had returned and their relationship was strengthened.

The above discussion, in a nutshell, shows the process behind this program. Following is a discussion of each of the three steps in the training process I mentioned earlier:

1. Opening the heart: This comes first because the heart is the symbolic seat of our emotions. It is in our hearts that we feel good when we are happy, in love, or joyful. It is here that we feel bad when we are sad, angry, and heartbroken. So I start by freeing the center of our feelings from the the restrictive impulses and influences that keep us from showing love for one another.

2. Surveying the emotional landscape: Once the basic heart-opening groundwork is done, you can look around and take note of the emotional terrain in which you live. You can learn to know just what you are feeling, how strongly, and why. You become aware of the ebb and flow of your emotions. You note the emotions being experienced by others and see how their feelings are affected by your actions. You begin to understand how all the emotions interact and sometimes create violent tides of feeling that roll over us and others. In short, you become wiser about your own feelings and those of people around you.

3. Taking responsibility: To bring about real and lasting changes in damaged relationships, you have to take responsibility. You can open your heart and map the emotional landscape of people around you, but that is not enough. When things go wrong between you and others, it is hard to fix the problem without going further. Everyone must define the problem, admit any faults and errors involved, make amends, and decide how to change things. Then, eventually the changes must be made.

People make mistakes in their relationships, little ones and big ones. When you make a mistake, you need to apologize and take responsibility for what you did. It also stands to reason that you should make amends and correct your behavior so the mistake won't happen again.

But these steps are easier said than done. Very few people are emotionally skilled enough to apologize sincerely, and without any defensiveness. It's easier to bypass the apology and take steps to avoid repeating the mistake. But that won't work nearly as well as when it follows an apology. However, most people are loath to admit, even to themselves, that they have done something wrong. If they can admit it to themselves, they have trouble admitting it to others. Others apologize freely and repeatedly but never do anything to change their behavior, so their apologies are meaningless. Taking responsibility for our actions and correcting our behavior is the final phase of emotional literacy training.

AN ENERGIZING PROCESS

What I have described may seem like a lot of work. You may think the process will drain you. In fact, it will energize you. We squander huge stocks of emotional energy when we block the expression of our emotions. Whether it's keeping silent about a shameful trauma, holding in our affectionate enthusiasm so as not to embarrass ourselves, or locking away a painful memory, we waste shocking amounts of energy repressing our feelings.

Letting go of these feelings not only releases the power of our emotions, it also gives us back the energy we wasted pushing them down. And letting others express their emotions brings them closer to us and saves us pain and heartache. That's why those who learn these lessons report such dramatic energy-enhancing effects.

It's an exciting prospect, isn't it? But we shouldn't rush forward blindly. Releasing our emotions can have complications. Feelings can get out of control and cause people to act impulsively. Therefore, it's best to go about liberating our emotions in a thoughtful and systematic way. I'll show you just how to do this using clearly explained, step-by-step exercises.

STRATEGIES OF
EMOTIONAL LITERACY TRAINING

If you practice the three emotional strategies discussed in this book—opening the heart, surveying the emotional landscape, and taking responsibility—you will see dramatic changes in your emotional awareness, attitude, and effectiveness.

In particular, you will learn:

- How to know what you want and what you feel; how to be truthful about your emotions; how to pursue fulfillment of your emotional needs.

- How to manage your emotions creatively; when to hold back and when to express your feelings.

- How to deal with emotional numbness or turmoil and get in touch with other people.

- How to apply your knowledge of emotions at work, at home, in school, in social groups, and "on the street" to improve and deepen your relationships and forge long-lasting, honest connections with people.

- How to practice a love-centered approach to personal power in a society that seems increasingly harsh and de-humanized.

WHERE TO START

What follows are the three stages each made up of four steps steps of emotional literacy training.

This set of emotionally literate transactions is arranged in order of difficulty.

You may find that you already have some skills in the first three or four steps and want to start at step five. Or, you may already be at step twelve but need to retune your skills. Either way is fine. But you should understand all the steps of emotional literacy training before you can begin to practice it effectively. If you don't know where you are going, it will be more difficult to find your way.

The following stages and steps of this process are like a road map to emotional transformation. Read them closely. They will help you see where you have been, where you are, and where you are going.

Here are the steps and stages that will be covered in detail in the chapters ahead:

Stage One: Opening the Heart

1. Giving Strokes

2. Asking for Strokes

3. Accepting and Rejecting Strokes

4. Giving Ourselves Strokes

Stage Two: Surveying the Emotional Landscape

5. Action/Feeling Statements

6. Accepting an Action/Feeling Statement

7. Revealing Our Intuitive Hunches

8. Validating an Intuitive Hunch

Stage Three: Taking Responsibility

9. Apologizing for Our Mistakes

10. Accepting or Rejecting Apologies

11. Asking for Forgiveness

12. Granting or Denying Forgiveness

SUMMARY

Training to Be Emotionally Literate

You don't have to go through life emotionally numb or tyrannized by your emotions. In the right environment, with supportive friends, family, or counselors, you can find a new emotional self.

You'll find the quest for a new emotional self exciting and satisfying. The process will energize you as you experience the power of your emotions and as you stop wasting energy to repress or hide them. To do so, you must practice with others who share your goal.

Opening the heart: With supportive friends, you take part in simple acts of mutual affection.

Surveying the emotional landscape: You focus on the ebb and flow of your own emotions and those of the people around you, listening with an open heart and striving to understand them.

Taking responsibility: You admit that you have made minor and major mistakes and hurt people in your relationships. You apologize and make amends.

4

STAGE ONE

OPENING THE HEART

An open heart is the foundation of Emotional Literacy and a requirement to effectively practice the next two stages of emotional literacy training: surveying the emotional landscape and taking responsibility.

In this portion of the training we apply what I learned from the original Stroke City exercise, namely that by the simple act of exchanging positive strokes we can cultivate and educate our loving capacities and allow our hearts to flourish. That is why the training starts here; by learning how to give and take affection.

THE POWER OF STROKES

People interact to get strokes. Strokes can be physical or verbal. Physical strokes are any form of touch: hugs, kisses, caresses, backrubs, holding hands or being held.

Verbal strokes are statements that acknowledge some feature of another person in a positive way. Verbal strokes can be about the person's looks, clothing, intelligence, generosity, creativity, emotional literacy, kindness, integrity, work ethic, practical skills, dignity, leadership ability, artistic talent, sexual responsiveness or prowess, honesty, playfulness, practical wisdom, elegance, tact, or any other attribute the person possesses.

The attributes that receive positive comment are not always so obvious or expected. For example, Jane has asked David to give her some strokes about something other than her looks. Jane is surprised when he tells her, "I envy the way you get so emotional. I wish I felt as sure about what I feel as you do. I like it that you have such strong emotions."

Jane had assumed that her tendency to cry at movies or during arguments was annoying. She was surprised (and pleased) to find that David admired her for this ability to show her emotions.

Of course, strokes are not always direct or spoken. Listening carefully as someone speaks or giving someone a bunch of flowers at the end of the week can be powerful strokes as well, "action strokes" if you will.

Marcel and Carrey are a good example of how important action strokes can be. Marcel is a very busy teacher. He has a full teaching schedule and a great deal of committee work. He brings work home from school and is always busy.

Marcel is not very good at giving verbal strokes, but Carrey his wife has accepted this shortcoming and his busy lifestyle because he is very good at giving her action strokes. He makes sure that when she needs to talk to him he pulls himself away from his work and listens with complete attention. He brings her breakfast in bed on weekends and he buys her little surprise presents. In short, he is constantly showing her affection with his actions in addition to the physical strokes they exchange whenever time permits. Even though Carrey would like to have longer conversations and more quality time with Marcel, she gives him action strokes just by being there and supporting him in his work.

They both feel well stroked, even though they exchange few verbal strokes and have very little time to be intimate.

Another example are Todd and Louis, two lifelong friends who exchange strokes almost exclusively at the action level. They get together regularly, talk about sports and cars, go fishing, have a beer or two. There is no question of their mutual affection and respect, and yet they never exchange physical strokes, and exchange verbal strokes only by complimenting each others' truck or prize catch. Both men get the strokes they need from their friendship. However, their wonderful friendship could be further improved if they opened their hearts more and learned to give each other verbal and even physical strokes.

Strokes can vary in their intensity or in the kind of reaction they cause. Some strokes are "superstrokes" because they are especially wanted. When I was a teenager, for example, I longed to hear that I was good-looking. It took years before I asked the question, and I was pleasantly surprised to hear the answer. A superstroke is also a stroke that comes from a special person, like a revered teacher, or our spouse or a person we have a crush on.

On the other hand, there are negative strokes. These can be obviously toxic insults, such as "Why can't you do anything right?" or subtle, hurtful remarks sometimes couched as jokes.

Negative strokes can be extremely damaging to a person's psyche. I have seen men who never got over being teased about their height as children, even though they grew to average size as adults. Tall girls frequently grow to become tall women who slump, simply because their schoolmates made fun of them.

Sometimes negative strokes can come disguised as compliments when they are based on a comparison between two people.

For example, Jean's mother frequently said to her, "You have all the looks in the family, but your sister Sara has all of the brains."

A statement like this was toxic to both of the girls, who came to resent their mother for pigeonholing them and each other as well. It took them years to realize that they were *both* good-looking and smart and that their mother had badly confused them with her devious compliment.

Another example of a stroke that could feel good but be

toxic would be a comparison such as, "You are my smartest relative." Again, this might *seem* like a positive stroke, but it is actually harmful, because it denigrates the other members of the family.

Sometimes a stroke that we do want can be delivered too strongly, making it unpleasant. An overly affectionate grandmother who smothers her grandchildren with kisses and a spouse who showers more attention on his wife than she may want are both examples of stroking gone awry.

Finally, strokes are sometimes given insincerely. These strokes are supposed to feel good but rarely do. They are called "plastic fuzzies" as opposed to "warm fuzzies." You may want to read *The Warm Fuzzy Tale*, my fairy tale about "warm fuzzies" and "cold pricklies" that makes these distinctions perfectly clear.

TROUBLE IN STROKE CITY

Our basic nature cries out for abundant strokes.

Unfortunately, positive strokes don't always flow freely, even among people who love one another. It should be simple and pleasurable both to give and to get them. But when most of us try to pass strokes back and forth, we fumble.

This vexing problem was exemplified by one of my clients, Thomas, who found that whenever he tried to say something loving to his wife his throat would constrict as if he were being choked by an invisible hand.

Though he knew what he wanted to say, he literally couldn't get the words out. On one occasion, when confronted by his wife's question, "Do you love me?", he did manage to force the words from his mouth. But all he could do was utter a barely understandable, froglike croak: "Ighh ghhluv ghuu."

Fortunately, his wife had a rich sense of humor, and much to his relief, burst out laughing.

"What?" she asked.

"I love you, I love you," he replied sheepishly, undercutting the powerful message by his hurried, embarrassed tone of voice.

This farcical example of a common problem shows the fear and even physical difficulty we run into when we try to speak about our loving emotions. People's evasions take many forms. "You know I love you," they may say. Or, "How many times do I have to tell you that I love you?" Or, "Would I be here if I didn't love you?"

Sometimes the sentiment is ruined just by the tone of voice—ironic, irritated, or dismissive: "Yes, dear, of course I love you." In any case, the loving stroke that one partner asked for has not truly been delivered. The speaker has avoided a full and honest expression of emotion.

This occurs commonly because few of us feel truly free to love openly. We are inhibited about giving, asking for, or accepting strokes. We are especially uptight about giving strokes to ourselves. What restricts us?

THE STROKE ECONOMY

There are unwritten rules about strokes. When we break these rules, people use disapproval or even harassment to enforce them.

If you warmly hug a loved one on a busy sidewalk, chances are that some people will look away uncomfortably. If you kiss or cuddle each other on a bus, other passengers may look embarrassed or frown. If you call your wife or husband from your office and say, "I love you," you open yourself up to remarks from the person at the next desk.

But these prohibitions don't come only from outsiders who disapprove. They are also severely enforced inside each of us by our inner Critical Parent.

What are these unwritten rules about giving and taking strokes? Where do they come from?

I first became aware of the prohibitions placed on stroking at one of Eric Berne's weekly meetings. At these meetings, we would try different "psychological experiments" as a form of recreation after our "scientific" meeting. On one occasion, I suggested we try one of the "games" played at that time by members of Synanon, a drug-treatment organization. In this game, group members would go at each other with savage criticism. They did this because they believed that the drug addict's character required that type of tough approach for change to happen. Following Synanon's example we went at it with glee, and the nasty comments—some offered supposedly in jest—flowed freely.

I found the experiment quite disturbing. My feelings had been hurt by some of the things said about me, but of course I did not tell the others of my distress. I would have been too embarrassed to admit how badly I'd been hurt, and how much I wanted the affection and respect of the group. Instead, I proposed that the next week we do just the opposite of what we had done and say positive, loving things about each other.

Everyone agreed. But at the next meeting, no one could think of much to say. Though we eventually muddled through, it was clear that producing positive strokes was hard, while producing negative ones was easy.

Not only were people inhibited about giving strokes, I discovered, but also about asking for them or even accepting them. Giving oneself strokes was definitely taboo.

Diana, a group therapy member, helped me see this. I noticed one afternoon that she seemed uneasy when someone in the group offered her a compliment. I asked her about her uneasiness.

"When Robert said something about me being pretty," she explained, "I was afraid that other people in the group might be thinking, 'I don't think so,' that if I smiled too much, or looked moved, they would think I looked needy and pathetic and pity me."

I suggested that, as an experiment, she ask Robert to give her the stroke again.

"But it would seem so pathetic and needy," she insisted, squirming in her chair.

Well, then, I suggested, how about giving yourself the same stroke? Tell yourself that you are pretty.

By now, there were tears in her eyes. When I asked her why she was crying, she admitted that Robert's compliment had shaken her up. She wanted to believe him and to thank him, but was terrified of allowing herself to look pleased.

I asked her to reflect on why she might be feeling this way. After thinking about it, she remembered that when she was in grammar school and high school, the unpopular kids were always most likely to be made fun of when they acted pleased with themselves.

Seeing this over and over had taught her to be afraid to accept strokes, especially a stroke that she really wanted. Doing that might cause her to become emotional in public and therefore, in her mind, make her seem ridiculous. Diana had no trouble giving strokes, but she had severe inhibitions against accepting them, asking for them, or giving them to herself.

Unfortunately, Diana was not an unusual case. Some of us reject any strokes that are given to us. Many of us, like Thomas, choke up when we try to deliver them. All of these reactions keep us from being close to people.

Have you ever felt a great desire to tell someone that you liked or loved them and found yourself unable to do so? Or have you found yourself wondering if a friend, family member, lover, or spouse really loves or likes you and, if so, in what way and for what reasons? Have you thought of coming right out and asking, only to dismiss the idea?

All of these are the result of our submission to the rules of the Stroke Economy.

THE STROKE ECONOMY RULES

The Stroke Economy is a set of rules enforced by our own Critical Parent, that critical voice we hear inside that keeps us from giving and accepting positive strokes. The Stroke Economy Rules that the Critical Parent would have us live by are these:

- Don't give strokes you want to give.

- Don't ask for strokes you want.

- Don't accept strokes you want.

- Don't reject strokes you don't want.

- Don't give yourself strokes.

WHY PEOPLE ACCEPT NEGATIVE STROKES

When people follow the dictates of the stroke economy the quantity of strokes exchanged is dramatically reduced. People will become stroke-starved. One very important and damaging side effect is that people begin to accept or even seek negative strokes because they can't get positive ones. In the same way that people dying of hunger or thirst will eat rotten food and drink polluted water, people will also accept and take in negative strokes when they can't get positive ones.

One of the most important discoveries I have made in the twenty years that I have been teaching Emotional Literacy is that by systematically breaking the rules of the Stroke Economy, and providing people with a steady diet of positive strokes people's hearts will automatically open. They will experience loving feelings they have not experienced before and the effect will spread out from them to their families and friends. I have seen many people develop their loving capacities over time simply by giving strokes, asking for strokes, accepting the strokes they want, rejecting the ones they don't want, and giving themselves strokes.

Let us begin with the first step: giving strokes.

STEP 1

Giving Strokes

Offering truthful statements of affection.

We feel love and the desire to give strokes at many levels—the subtle touch of warmth for a neighbor's child, fondness for an old friend, the longing to merge with a lover. But these strokes often go unspoken.

The first step is giving strokes, but before you start giving strokes, let me explain some ground rules for all the Emotional Literacy exercises that will be presented in this book.

- Ask for permission. Be respectful of others' boundaries and feelings.

- Be honest. Truthfulness is a basic requirement of Emotional Literacy.

- Stand up against your Critical Parent.

ASK FOR PERMISSION

Any emotional communication can be a strong experience.

It is not uncommon in emotional literacy training to see people cry when they are given a much desired stroke, asked a particular question, or given a needed apology.

But there are other reasons besides strong emotional response for asking the other person's permission to speak about strokes or any other emotional issues:

- to give the other person a warning that a difficult communication is coming.

- to give people a chance to prepare and be ready to listen.

- to give the other person a choice about whether he or she wants to discuss the issue at this time (the person may have a splitting headache or a big exam in the morning);

When we follow this approach, we are ensuring that our statements will fall on fertile soil and will have a chance to generate productive responses.

By asking for permission every time we are about to engage in an emotion-laden transaction we are avoiding possible shock, defensiveness, fear, and even anger in the other person.

Most important, though, the recipient has to be given a genuine choice. We need to be willing to accept that the timing of our statement might not be particularly good and, if so, be willing to wait for a better moment.

By going slow and easy, we prepare ourselves and the other person for the deeply emotional response that might occur.

This is done in the most basic way. Whenever you are planning to give a stroke, or address an emotional issue, you should always prepare the person by asking if it is okay.

Give him or her an idea of what you are about to say with a comment like: "Can I tell you something I like about you?" or "I would like to talk about a feeling I had when we talked the other night," or "I have been wanting to apologize to you for something I said a while ago."

Some further examples of asking permission:

- "May I tell you what my favorite thing about you is?"

- "I have been feeling upset lately. May I explain?"

- "There is something going on between us that I don't like. Are you interested in talking about it?"

Being emotionally literate takes courage, and it can seem too scary to try. If you want to learn to give strokes for instance, start with simpler tasks: "May I say something to you?" followed by a small compliment, and work your way up. As you get more comfortable and better at it, you'll find that those seemingly insolvable and intimidating situations will become fewer and fewer; you will know how to rise to the occasion and say what you want to say.

Many people fear that these preambles are awkward. That is because what needs to be done is unusual and sometimes seems unnatural and likely to be ridiculed. Emotional discourse can be dismissed as "psychobabble" or laughed at by people who are uncomfortable with their emotions.

Nonetheless, these are important methods that produce the changes we are trying to make.

Although asking permission to make any kind of emotion-laden statement might seem strange, practice will remove this strangeness over time. Eventually, this seemingly odd ritual will become second nature. You will become emotionally literate enough to know which occasions require formal permission and when you can just go ahead and give the stroke.

BE HONEST

Throughout this book the theme of honesty will come up, over and over again. The fact is that heart-based Emotional Literacy cannot develop in an environment of lies or subtle dishonesty. In order for people to feel the trust and confidence in each other needed to acquire the skills that I teach here, they have to make a commitment to truthfulness and honesty. (See Notes for Philosophers; Lying and Truthfulness.) Giving strokes is the first opportunity to practice the principle of truthfulness.

A stroke has to be honest, not manufactured. Anything else will be confusing and counterproductive.

As our hearts open, so do our intuitive powers. It is confusing to our intuition to receive a stroke that is presented as heartfelt and sincere but instead feels phony and unreal.

When we decide to give a stroke we must make sure that it is authentic. For some people honesty is easy because they

73

know how they truly feel. For others, that is where the learning begins.

For instance, Daphne was taught early in life that being nice and saying nice things to people was important.

After years of saying nice things and never considering their truth, Daphne doesn't really know how she feels about people or what it is that she likes or doesn't like about them. Because of that, she has to concentrate to become aware of her true feelings.

Sometimes, when she is being truthful with herself, she realizes that she has nothing complimentary to say. When that happens, she cannot honestly give a verbal stroke. At such times her Critical Parent makes her feel very guilty, and she reverts to the values she was raised with and invents a stroke, whether she feels it or not. By doing this, she misses seeing that simply listening to people, touching them lightly, or smiling can be a stroke as well; an action stroke, as I have explained.

What Daphne should do is sit back and tune in to how she feels and resist the nagging of her Critical Parent who urges her to "Say something nice, stupid!" Unless she is true to herself, she cannot be true to others. And others intuit when she is not telling the truth.

STAND UP
AGAINST YOUR CRITICAL PARENT

The main problem in giving strokes is our Critical Parent, who acts like an emotional prison guard giving us discouraging messages that keep us from getting in touch with our true feelings. Here are some of the messages our Critical Parent whispers or shouts that stop us from giving strokes:

- If the stroke is not wanted by the other person, I will look foolish.

- The stroke I have is inappropriate, badly worded, and clumsy. If I say it, I will only make a fool of myself.

- It will seem like a sexual advance.

- It will just seem like insincere politeness anyway, so why take the risk?

- Someone will think I am needy or desperate for friendship.

- If I get overemotional, I will just make everyone feel awkward, and then I might get upset. For example, "If I tell my sister that I really miss her, I might start crying. Then she'll be embarrassed, I'll be embarrassed, and we'll both feel stupid. Better to just say, 'It's good ta see ya!' and leave it at that."

By courageously addressing these feelings and giving strokes in spite of them, we engage in the ongoing battle with our Critical Parent.

As we see the appreciation for our strokes we begin to get strokes back and we feed our strong hunger for strokes. We realize how wrong the Stroke Economy Rules really are. When that happens, the voice of the Critical Parent gradually loses its power to inhibit us.

For example, Melanie is shy about giving strokes and she wishes she could be more generous with them. She would like to give some strokes to her friend, Janelle, who is moving away to New York.

She tells Janelle that she thinks her new hairstyle is really gorgeous. "You should keep it like that!" Melanie says enthusiastically. To her surprise, Janelle laughs nervously and says nothing. "Seriously, it's perfect for you," Melanie adds. Still no response.

Having stuck her neck out to give a sincere stroke, Melanie is hurt and disappointed. Later, thinking about it, she realizes that she gave that stroke abruptly without asking for permission. Maybe Janelle is uneasy about her appearance and doesn't believe Melanie's flattering remarks.

She resolves to ask for permission the next time.

The next time they talk, after Janelle has just told a very funny joke, Melanie mentions "You know something?" she says, still laughing.

"What?"

"May I tell you something I like about you?"

"Okay." Janelle says, wanly.

"I really like your sense of humor. At least we can still laugh together on the phone after you move."

Janelle smiles, looking a little sad. Finally, Melanie has hit on a stroke that Janelle is able to respond to.

Emboldened by her success, Melanie addresses Janelle.

"May I tell you something else? You know, you're like a sister to me; I'm going to miss you so much!"

Now Janelle doesn't know what to say. She smiles nervously, then looks serious. She promises to call as soon as she arrives in New York.

Again, Melanie is disappointed. What went wrong? Does Janelle feel guilty for leaving? Do emotional good-byes make her self-conscious? She goes out and buys a card for Janelle. She writes:

Dear Janelle,

I had the feeling last night that when I said you were like a sister to me and I'll miss you, I made you uncomfortable. I'm not sure how you took what I said, but all that's important to me is that I let you know what a great time I always have with you, and how smart and funny I think you are. Best wishes in your new home.

To Melanie's delight Janelle wrote her a postcard two weeks later:

Dear Melanie,

Got your sweet card. I love you too. Very busy. Let's stay in touch.

Your New York sister,
Janelle

76

By starting out slowly and learning to ask for permission, and then by using written communication to give herself and Janelle some breathing room to get over their feelings of self-consciousness, Melanie was gradually learning the ropes of exchanging strokes. She was desensitizing herself to the initial fear and awkwardness and working her way up from simple to more profound expressions of positive, loving emotion.

Over time, both she and Janelle became more free in their ability to give and receive affection. This happened because Melanie decided that she wanted to give Janelle strokes and was not dissuaded by either her own Critical Parent or Janelle's initial inability to receive them.

With practice, it will become easier and easier. Start small and work your way up.

THE POETRY OF STROKES

A stroke should be a love poem. Brief and shy, perhaps, or full throated and showy. One word or a long paragraph, but always from the heart and always hopeful and sincere. Even if it is an action stroke without words or physical contact, a stroke works because it is an act of kindness and love extended to another person. To open up our hearts we need to examine our lives and ask ourselves how many times in a day we actually perform this basic function of human nature; expressing love to another person almost imperceptibly, passionately or somewhere in between, whether within our family, at work or on the street. And if we discover, as is often the case, that we are depriving others of our love, we must resolve to do something about it and then go ahead and against all odds, do it.

STEP 2

Asking for Strokes

Asking for strokes that we need.

It's nice to get strokes, but sometimes they aren't available or the ones that are available are not the ones we want.

We can spend years silently and timidly waiting to learn whether the people in our lives think we are smart, creative, good-looking, or kind. We try to guess if they find these positive qualities in us. We never simply ask. We have become so obedient to the Critical Parent that the idea doesn't even occur to us. But there are times when we need to ask for strokes. At that point we need to decide what to ask for and from whom.

Asking for strokes is riskier than giving them.

We can never be completely sure that the strokes we want are going to come our way. The other person may not honestly be able to tell us what we would like to hear. It is therefore more hazardous to ask for a specific stroke ("Do you like the way I sing?" or "Will you give me a hug?") than to ask for any stroke a person may have, physical or verbal.

The risk of the latter request is that we might get a stroke we don't want. The reality is that in most situations, when we ask, we can get what we need. For example:

"Hi, Daphne. I'm having a really bad day. I feel embarrassed saying this, but I could really use some moral support about my writing. Do you have any strokes that you can give me?"

Such conversations are normally complicated, made almost impossible because people expect each other to lie out of politeness. That's why it's so important to find good friends, or a lover or spouse, someone who will be honest and gentle. The most important step toward Emotional Literacy is finding someone to learn it with.

Once you have found a person who is interested in an affectionate, thoughtful dialogue you can say things like:

"I just bought these pants. Do you like them? Do you think that I look good in them?"

Or:

"I wrote a letter to the editor of the newspaper. Would you read it and tell me if you like it?"

Or:

"I just had a tough conversation with my teenager. I'm feeling unsure about being a good father. Can you give me some strokes about my parenting?"

Or:

"I looked at myself in the mirror this morning and I can see some new wrinkles in my face. I'm afraid I'm becoming old and ugly. Can you tell me something you like about my face?"

Or:

"I've been feeling very lonely at this party. Everyone is having such a good time. Do you want to dance with me?"

STEP 3

Accepting and Rejecting Strokes

Accepting strokes we want and rejecting strokes that we do not want.

We all need strokes in much the same way that we need food. When we get stroke-starved, complications can occur. We may become confused about what strokes to take or to reject.

We may be stroke-starved because we simply are not getting any strokes to speak of. But often we are in need of strokes because we refuse to take the strokes that are available. We may be very particular about the strokes we want and refuse all others, or we may develop a sort of stroke anorexia and voluntarily starve ourselves of them. Finally, strokes may be offered to us which are toxic, but seem attractive.

Given all these complications, we are very likely to discount all or part of most of the strokes we get even if they are positive and needed. We may:

- say "thank you" but shrug the stroke off with a smile.

- quickly reciprocate with another stroke, not allowing the stroke we were given to soak in ("Thank you, I think your shoes are really nice too.")

- actually argue with the stroke and minimize it ("Oh, no, saving your life was easy; anyone would have done it.").

Very often the rejection of a stroke is done internally, while one outwardly appears to accept it.

In these cases the rejection is often betrayed by revealing gestures and physical attitudes—a shrug, a somber look, a shaking of the head, a doubtful, puzzled look, or a nervous smile. All these are outward signs that we are pretending to accept the stroke. Internally, however, we are really listening to our Critical Parent tell us that we shouldn't accept it.

When we are told that we are good-looking, passionate, smart, intense, funny, soulful, compassionate, charismatic, or easygoing and good-natured, we are prevented from enjoying the stroke by our Critical Parent, who tells us:

- The person doesn't know us and therefore can't be taken seriously.

- Even if the person does know us, there is something dark and hidden about us that makes the stroke undeserved.

- The stroke is just an attempt to be polite or a charitable effort to make us feel better.

- The stroke is more deserved by someone else, so we should not be allowed to take it.

- Accepting strokes is immodest and conceited.

- We will embarrass ourselves if we accept the stroke.

- We will become emotional in public and make others uncomfortable.

- We are accepting the stroke too easily, that we are stroke-starved and needy, and therefore too desperate for praise.

CASE STUDY IN ACCEPTANCE

In one of my training workshops, after I explained the Stroke Economy and established the cooperative ground rules (No power plays or attempts to manipulate and no lies. See Introduction, page 8), I invited the participants to go ahead and break the rules of the Stroke Economy.

A thoughtful quiet ensued. After some of the people gave and took strokes for a while, Anna began to talk about how she had plenty of permission to give strokes but no permission to take them. I asked her if she wanted to do something about it. Shyly she agreed, and I asked her what she wanted to do. "I would like to give everyone here a stroke," she said.

I responded that this would be very nice but it might be a bit too easy for her. How about asking everybody to give *her* a stroke? She was puzzled by the idea and shook her head.

"Well, in that case what if just one person here gave you a stroke?

After some thought she nodded: "Okay," she said.

"I think you should ask," I said. She found this very difficult but eventually said to the group, "I would like a stroke from anyone here."

Valery eagerly offered.

"I am so glad you asked, can I give you a stroke?"

"Okay," said Anna.

"I have known you for some years now, and what I like about you most is how sweet and loving you are."

Anna's face darkened. "Thank you," she said.

I saw that the stroke had not worked.

"Can I ask you, Anna, did you take that stroke?" I asked.

Thinking about it, she said no. She explained that while she heard the stroke she also heard her Critical Parent say "She really doesn't know you. That sweetness is just an act, always being nice, never being yourself."

I turned to Valery and asked her if she agreed that she didn't know Anna. Valery responded.

"I know that sometimes she doesn't speak her mind, but she is extremely loving, and I know that for a fact."

Turning to Anna I asked if she believed Valery and Anna nodded yes. "You know what, Anna?" I asked. Anna looked at me curiously. "I think to do this right you need to apologize to Valery. She offered you this heartfelt stroke, and instead you listened to your Critical Parent and rejected her stroke. Would you consider apologizing and ask her to give you the stroke again?"

Anna agreed. She apologized and asked for the stroke again. This time she heard it and smiled happily and took a deep breath as a warm blush spread over her cheeks.

Clearly, Anna had leaped a big hurdle and everyone was moved.

When we give a stroke and suspect that it hasn't been fully accepted, it is important to investigate: "Did you hear what I said? Do you accept it? Do you believe me?

"It seems that you did not quite take in my compliment, am I right?"

It may be quite a struggle to convince someone to take a heartfelt stroke, but it is worth the effort. Giving a stroke that is rejected or discounted can be embarrassing and disappointing for both parties, so it is reasonable to gently persist:

- "Please take the compliment. I really mean it."

- "Didn't you like what I said? Why? Is there some other way I can phrase it?"

Keep in mind that for stroke-starved people, strokes sometimes act like water on a parched houseplant. At first they may sit on the surface and go nowhere, but eventually they soak into the soil and nourish the recipient. Sometimes the process must be repeated before there is any effect.

Because of this, it is important to watch people as you give them strokes. You can tell from their behavior if the stroke is going in or is being rejected. A deep breath or a quietly happy look are the best signs that a stroke has been heard and, more important, taken.

REJECTING UNWANTED STROKES

The most obvious example of unwanted strokes is sexual strokes from someone we are not interested in. Most people can attest that it is very hard to reject unwanted sexual strokes. A woman may be unable to reject a sexual comment because she feels it would be impolite to ask the person to stop. Learning to reject unwanted strokes is an important skill—we need to stop the unwanted stroke to avoid a more uncomfortable or even damaging situation.

Furthermore, when adults or older children impose sexual strokes on younger children or adolescents, those strokes are undeniably harmful.

Curiosity and hunger for attention can result in a child seeming to consent to sexual strokes, which later prove to be emotionally harmful. When we teach kids about molestation, we are essentially teaching them how to reject damaging strokes and, if necessary, get away from (and report) someone who won't take no for an answer.

There are other unwanted strokes that are less obvious than the ones mentioned above. These are not toxic strokes; rather, they are strokes that seem to limit us.

For example, a beautiful woman may eventually tire of being told she's beautiful. When that stroke is offered to her, it may make her feel one-dimensional, as though that is all anyone ever notices about her. If she thinks that the affection of others is based only on her beauty, then she may feel trapped into always playing the part of the pretty woman.

Actually, she may be starved to have attention paid to her ideas, her work, or her integrity. With emotional literacy training, she would learn to explain:

"I'm sorry but I've been feeling lately that you only compliment me for my looks. I guess I feel neglected in other ways. For instance, I really wanted you to congratulate me on my job promotion. But I know you don't mean to offend or disappoint me. Instead of strokes about my looks could you give me other strokes instead?"

Similarly, a hard-working man who is constantly praised for his hard work and responsibility may tire of such praise.

Perhaps he would like to have more fun, and he feels that he is only appreciated for his willingness to work. Or perhaps he has other talents or admirable qualities that he feels no one notices, such as being good with his kids.

When people begin to resent a stroke they often receive, they usually think they must always play the same old role to be appreciated. It's important to listen carefully if someone asks us for a different stroke, and support his or her honesty.

Of course, rejecting an unwanted stroke can be uncomfortable and possibly even damage your relationship with the other person. After all, when a person gives you a compliment from the heart, he or she expects to hear at least a thank you.

In these cases it is important to decline the stroke gracefully. In an open hearted manner explain why, and state what you would rather hear and ask for the stroke you really want.

SEPARATING WHEAT FROM CHAFF

The most difficult task in this enterprise is separating the strokes we want from those we don't want, and separating the strokes that are good for us from those that may be harmful.

When we don't seem to want a certain stroke we need to ask ourselves: "Do I reject this stroke because it is bad for me or is this a perfectly good stroke that my Critical Parent doesn't want me to have?"

When we decide that the stroke offered is good and we want it, we must fight our Critical Parent and accept it. If we figure out that it is bad or redundant, then we should reject it.

Lately there has been a society-wide movement to help people reject strokes they don't want. This is a very positive development that protects mostly women and children from the damage unwanted strokes can cause.

The negative side of this movement is that we have built up additional barriers against all sorts of strokes. People are afraid that their heartfelt strokes will be misinterpreted and they will be perceived as being harmful or that in some cases simply holding a crying child or being friendly with a coworker will be construed as sexual behavior.

This new stroke phobia is most evident in the way people who work with children are now refraining from any physical affection, no matter how innocuous. This fear of prosecution reinforces the ill effects of the Stroke Economy and contributes greatly to the current emotional numbing of people and an increase in social alienation and depression.

This is why it has become even more important to teach this distinction between the strokes we want and are good for us from the strokes that are bad and should be rejected.

STEP 4

Giving Ourselves Strokes

Adding to our confidence through healthy self-love.

While there is no real substitute for getting strokes from others, knowing how to give yourself strokes is an important skill that is very useful when we get into a difficult situation away from people who will stroke us.

Most of us have been conditioned to think of "patting ourselves on the back" as immodest and conceited or even needy, foolish, and humiliating.

There is nothing to be embarrassed about in giving yourself strokes even if you are not in great need of them. There may be things about yourself that others do not know, or perhaps people in your life have been stingy with their strokes and you need more than you are getting.

It is perfectly all right to give yourself strokes, very good, in fact.

For instance, after everyone had devoured a great meal that Colin made, he looked around the table and asked, "Well, did you like the meal?"

Everyone nodded and grunted appreciatively, but offered little in the way of detailed response.

Somewhat disappointed by the lack of praise, Colin said, "Well, if you ask me, I thought the chicken was really tender and the rice was spicy and fluffy. I worked very hard to make it like that. I can see you all enjoyed it. I'm really happy."

"Are you upset with us? We really did like it. I know I did," said Carrie, worried that Colin was reprimanding them for their meager responses.

"No, no, I was just giving myself a little pat on the back for a job well done," he declared. The others smiled approvingly, and everyone felt good about the exchange.

FIGHTING THE CRITICAL PARENT

We especially need to be able to stroke ourselves to counteract the negative strokes we get from our Critical Parent, telling us that we are stupid, bad, crazy, ugly, or doomed. For this we need to understand how to respond when our Critical Parent attacks us.

If your Critical Parent says that you are stupid and unreliable and can't be trusted, you need to be able to contradict this slander and tell yourself something like: "I am intelligent and a high achiever. Considering the fact that I have two well-cared for children at home, I know I am reliable and can be trusted. I am proud of how smart, reliable, and trustworthy I am."

If your Critical Parent says that you are fat, ugly, and doomed, you need to be able to say, "So I don't have the looks of a model. But I have a nice healthy body and people have told me they find me handsome and attractive. I like the way I look and I am sure that I will meet the right partner for me."

In Transactional Analysis the source of this kind of positive "self talk" is called the "Nurturing Parent."

Certain people are able to preserve a bedrock compassion toward themselves, despite criticism and ridicule from peers and their Critical Parent. This healthy self-love suggests a well-established, core confidence supported by the Nurturing Parent.

SUMMARY

Opening the Heart

We start this exercise because the Heart is at the seat of the emotions. We open our hearts and strengthen our bonds with others by giving and receiving strokes.

We all need positive strokes. There are physical strokes, such as hugs and kisses; verbal strokes, such as compliments about our looks, intelligence, kindness, integrity, or taste; and action strokes, such as being attentive or helpful or showing empathy or affection.

The Stroke Economy is a set of rules that prevents us from giving and asking for strokes, accepting the strokes we want, and rejecting the ones we don't want. It also prevents us from giving ourselves strokes. The result is that we become stroke-starved and are willing to take whatever strokes we can get.

By releasing ourselves from the rules of the Stroke Economy, we free ourselves to be loving with each other, and satisfy our need for strokes. To do this we have to disobey the Critical Parent inside of us, which enforces the rules of the Stroke Economy and interferes with every attempt to gain Emotional Literacy.

We learn how to give people the strokes they want. We ask for the strokes we want. We learn how to accept or reject strokes. To do this we must figure out whether we want or don't want a certain stroke that is offered.

When rejecting a stroke we must make sure we don't really want it. It's difficult to reject a stroke when we are stroke-starved. That is one reason why we need to learn to ask for and accept strokes we want. This keeps us stroke-nourished so that we are not tempted to take toxic strokes.

We should reject toxic strokes, but when our Critical Parent prevents us from taking a stroke we want we should defy this prohibition.

Finally, we learn to develop our Nurturing Parent and give ourselves strokes to build our self confidence.

5

SURVEYING THE EMOTIONAL LANDSCAPE

We can argue about the nature and purpose of our emotions and even whether they are our friends or enemies. We cannot argue, however, with their existence.

They affect us every minute of the day, whether we know it or not.

Many of us may be numb to our emotions, a few too sensitive to them. We may be afraid of them or too ready to embrace them.

How to become aware of our emotions and the emotions of others is the subject of this section. Here we will learn to recognize, map out and navigate the emotional terrain.

The causes of our emotions are often unclear. We tend to think of them as irrational, but that is a serious mistake. Every emotion we have has a definite cause and is usually related to someone else's behavior. We need to understand these causes if we are to be emotionally literate.

In the last two decades popular psychology has led us to believe that we cannot cause feelings in others. You may have come to believe this false idea which gained a foothold when psychologist Fritz Perls wrote his "Gestalt Prayer," a poem that eventually was recited at thousands of human potential workshops across the Western World.

> *I do my thing, and you do your thing.*
> *I am not in this world to live up to your expectations*
> *And you are not in this world to live up to mine.*
> *You are you and I am I,*
> *If by chance we find each other, it's beautiful.*
> *If not, it can't be helped.*

I believe that with his poem, Perls was trying to help people rid themselves of the excessive and guilt-based demands that people often make on themselves and each other. However, what he wrote became vulgarized into a call for emotional irresponsibility. In essence, it supported the belief that we are not responsible for the way others feel.

The mistaken belief that we cannot make one another feel is the high point of emotional illiteracy. Years ago, I was so disturbed by the misguided implications in Perls's poem, that I wrote a response to it.

> *If I do my thing and you do your thing*
> *And if we don't live up to each other's expectations*
> *We might live but the world will not survive.*
> *You are you, and I am I, and together,*
> *Joining hands, not by chance,*
> *We will find each other beautiful.*
> *If not, we can't be helped.*

What I was trying to say here is obvious to most feeling people. We are responsible for each other. Regarding emotions, we can indeed cause them in each other, and therefore we are often responsible for other people's feelings.

However, there are those who vehemently disagree. At a lecture in which I was presenting my point of view on the subject, a man stood up and interrupted me.

"I completely disagree with you," he exclaimed. "You cannot make me feel anything unless I let you."

I am embarrassed to admit that I took his bait. Faking anger, I stared at him and said: "That is the stupidest thing I have ever heard! Sit down!"

Stunned by my response, he turned bright red and sat down. From where I stood, he appeared to be scared and very sad.

"Now, may I ask you something?" I asked. "What are you feeling right now?"

"Nothing," he insisted.

I was bewildered by his response. He was obviously shaken, yet he insisted that he was not. I turned to the rest of the audience and asked: "How about you? Did anybody feel anything?"

Many hands shot up. One by one people voiced their feelings. I had made some of them angry. Others were embarrassed, while others felt afraid. Even though my abusive breach of ethics left me very uneasy, I had proven my point. A number of people had been made to feel strong emotions by my staged response to this man.

Clearly, if people can be made to feel fear, anger, shame, and other negative emotions, then they can also be made to feel the emotions of joy, love, pride, and hope. That is ultimately what achieving Emotional Literacy is all about; giving people the tools to move from emotional numbness or frightening chaos to a positive, heart-centered, emotionally balanced life.

In this stage of the training we explore emotional awareness, which is the understanding of how emotions affect us every day. We will examine what we feel and what others feel, how strongly we feel those feelings, and why. The goal of this stage is to make us comfortable and well-oriented in the "emotional landscape." We will look at:

- The connection between a person's feelings and his or her own actions, and

- The connection between one person's actions and another person's feelings.

Both of these points relate to the fact that actions and feelings are closely related to each other and can't be kept apart. Our actions can cause feelings in the people around us which in turn can cause them to act in ways which will cause feelings in us and so on, and so on. This cycle of feelings and actions can be positive and constructive, or it can be destructive and vicious.

It is the connection between actions and feelings that we are looking at in this next step.

STEP 5

Action/Feeling Statements

Finding a way of talking about your feelings that does not involve judgments, accusations, or theories.

As a method of exploring the connection between actions and feelings I want to introduce you to a new tool: the *action/feeling statement.*

An action/feeling statement is a one-sentence description of the emotions we feel as the result of another person's action. The boilerplate version of this transaction is as follows:

"When you (action), I felt (emotion)."

Very simple, isn't it? This statement is designed to tell another person about a feeling you had because of his or her behavior. It also helps to avoid placing blame or making someone defensive by staying away from any judgments or accusations.

An action/feeling statement simply says that the action of one person resulted in an undeniable feeling in another.

ACTION/FEELING CASE STUDY

John and Mary have a telephone conversation that Mary ends abruptly. John is upset by this sudden disconnection. The next day he calls Mary to tell her how her action made him feel. He asks if he can tell her something that is troubling him, and she agrees to listen to it.

"When you wanted to stop talking on the phone last night, I felt angry at first, and then sad."

Assuming that Mary can agree that she ended the telephone conversation abruptly, she now understands that John felt sad and angered by her action. This action/feeling statement successfully provides Mary with information about how John felt when she hung up.

A small goal you might say, but a critically important one in the learning of Emotional Literacy. It was also successful in that it was a way for John to express his feelings so that he did not hurt or abuse Mary.

In an emotionally literate relationship, no emotional event is too small to be discounted. Invariably once these seemingly trivial emotional events are explored, they reveal deeper emotional issues—personal insecurities or recurrent inequities in a relationship.

A single action/feeling statement shows that an action resulted in a particular feeling. A series of action/feeling exchanges will have a dramatically clarifying effect on any emotional conflict.

The reason for this is that action/feeling statements are a means of dissecting an emotional conflict, section by section. This is done by separating a conflict into two elements: *What happened* and *what you felt*.

Action/feeling statements are not as easy to exchange as it

might seem. Errors can be made. For example, confusing action with motivation and confusing thoughts for feelings.

Confusing Action with Motivation. When attempting to describe an action, it is possible to go beyond a simple statement, such as:

- "When you hung up the telephone"
- "When you arrived late"
- "When you interrupted me,"

and add to it a judgment or interpretation of the action being described, such as:

- "When you *so rudely* hung up on me"
- "When you *humiliated* me by being late"
- "When you *showed your disregard* for my opinion by interrupting me."

These ideas put forward a theory about the other person's motivation (the intent to humiliate or disregard), rather than a simple description of an action.

Elaborations like these confuse matters. They are often incorrect, and invariably create unnecessary guilt, anger, and other explosive feelings.

It's best to save these elaborations for later when you are asked to express your intuitions. For now we are dealing with the connection between one person's actions and another person's feelings.

Confusing Feelings with Thoughts. Another error that can occur in an action/feeling statement is confusing feeling and thinking.

When we try to express a feeling, we often state a thought instead. For instance: "When you interrupted our conversation,

94

I felt *that you were angry*," or "When you interrupted our conversation, I felt *that you weren't interested* in what I had to say."

These are not feelings at all. Like the interpretations we looked at above, they are really theories about what was going on in the other person's mind. Literacy has to do with language, and to confuse a feeling with an idea, thought, or theory is a common mistake that we need to avoid.

To construct a good action/feeling statement, you need to focus on what *you* feel, not what you suspect or assume that the other person was thinking or feeling because that is the only thing you can know for sure: how you feel. If you want to know how others feel you have to ask and make sure.

Many arguments between people are based on this type of false assumption. For instance, Frances believes that her husband doesn't look up from the paper when she talks because he isn't interested in what she has to say. Actually, he is interested. The problem is that he tries to read and listen to her at the same time, something that doesn't work very well in most cases. What *is* true is that when he splits his attention in that way she feels sad and eventually, very angry.

Another more subtle version of this confusion of feeling with thought is a statement like: "When you interrupted our conversation, I felt rejected."

This is an error too, since rejection is not really an emotion but, again, a theory about the other person's motivation to reject you. It does not explain to your listener what *you* are *feeling*. Were you angry? Were you sad? Were you embarrassed? Were you ashamed? These are feelings. Rejection is not.

When you say that you felt rejected, you are really saying that the other person rejected you, a theory about the person's motivation that may be incorrect.

All the above errors involve either laying blame or trying to read the mind of the other person. Action/feeling statements teach us to stick to the facts and to stop assuming we can read other people's minds.

Keep the action/feeling statement simple: What happened and how you felt.

Opinions vary on the definitive list of basic primary emotions. Fortunately for all practical purposes we have a pretty good idea that anger, fear, sadness, shame, and hatred are primary negative emotions while love, pride, and joy are primary positive emotions. Jealousy, guilt, envy, hopelessness, and hope are secondary combinations of basic emotions. When speaking about them we should try to break them down into their primary component parts. For instance, if Sam is feeling guilty, it might be helpful if he realized that his guilt is made up of shame and fear. Daria could explain her emotions more clearly when she is envious if she could specify that her primary emotions are anger, sadness and fear.

On the other hand, if a person says he feels humiliated, discounted, rejected, insulted or loved for instance, those are definitely not emotions but statements about what others are doing to him. They need to be reevaluated and the hidden emotional response needs to be discovered and stated.

Is sex an emotion? How about hunger or thirst? Are psychological pain and hurt emotions? As of this writing, I am not sure. It remains to be seen. That should not prevent us from continuing to pursue Emotional Literacy by stating actions and feelings in as clear a manner as possible.

EXTRACTING AN ACTION/FEELING STATEMENT

Sometimes you may need to help a person clarify how he or she felt when you did something. To do this successfully you will have to ignore judgments and accusations and help shape what is being said into the action/feeling mold. It is especially important to listen carefully and intuitively to understand the other person's feelings.

In the above case of Mary and John, let's pretend that John said, "When you so rudely hung up yesterday, I felt that you didn't care about me at all."

In order to extract a workable action/feeling statement from this comment, Mary might respond, "Now wait, let me get this straight. You are saying that when I stopped our conversation yesterday, which I remember doing, you felt something. But I can't tell what it was you felt. Were you angry?"

"No, I felt you were being rude."

"Okay, you thought I was being rude, but would you be willing to tell me how you felt? I am interested in how you felt at the time."

"I don't know. I felt that you didn't like me."

"Well, O.K. but you still haven't told me how you felt."

"What do you mean?"

"I am trying to figure out what feeling, what emotion you felt. What were you feeling that made you think I didn't like you? Were you sad?"

"A bit. Actually, yeah, very sad. Then I started to feel angry."

"Okay, now I know what I wanted to know. You felt sad and angry."

By now, dear reader, you may be saying: "People don't talk like that in the real world. Maybe they do in California, but not anywhere else. I'm not willing to talk like that. I'd be embarrassed to death."

That's a fine action/feeling statement. "When speaking in an emotionally literate way, I feel embarrassment."

I recognize the problem and can only agree with you. People don't usually talk this way and it is embarrassing and very difficult at times.

But it works. It creates a favorable climate for rational, emotional expression. It cools down unruly feelings, gives people an opportunity to express these emotions that is less likely to result in further upset, and lays the groundwork for safe and productive emotional dialogue. It lets others know that how they feel is important to us—that we listen to them and value them enough to have an honest exchange. It informs people of one another's emotional topography so that they can more easily find their way around it in the future.

STEP 6

Accepting an Action/Feeling Statement

**Developing a nondefensive acceptance of the emotional
information being given.**

To be effective, an emotionally literate communication must be
received as well as sent.

When you are the recipient of an action/feeling statement, the
emotionally literate thing to do is to take careful note of the emotions being described and your action that triggered them.

This can be very difficult. The biggest problem is that when we
are told that we may have made a mistake or that we have made
another person feel bad we are likely to respond with guilt and
defensiveness. Our first impulse will be to deny, explain, justify or
even apologize. But instead, I want to emphasize, it is important
to simply absorb the information that is being given: The emotions
caused in another person by your actions.

The point is not how bad or wrong you were to act the way
you did, but how what you did made the other person feel. Nor is
it that you should apologize immediately or explain why you did
what you did. The point is understanding the connection between
your action and what the other person felt. Remember, we are
interested in understanding how we affect each other emotionally,
rather than placing responsibility or blame. Taking responsibility is
important, but it comes later, after we understand each other well
enough to apologize and make amends meaningfully and effectively.

Mary, to use the above example, may already know that her
abrupt termination of the telephone call left John feeling angry and
sad, or she might be surprised. She may understand why he feels
this way, or she may be puzzled by it. In any case, all she needs
to do for now is to listen carefully, get the information, and acknowledge it. This acknowledgment can be in the form of a nod,
or by saying, "I hear you," or "I understand that when I ended

the conversation, you felt sad, and then angry, or I just don't under-stand."

By doing this, Mary learns about John's emotional responses to different types of situations, and she gives him an opportunity to let go of his bad feelings. This begins the process of emotional dialogue in which feelings are given proper recognition.

Again, accepting an action/feeling statement is not easy. The danger in receiving an action/feeling statement, especially if it is imperfectly formulated, is triggering a defensive response and say-ing something like:

- "I thought you were finished talking; that's why I wanted to stop," or

- "Rude? What's so rude about ending a conversation? You were being rude by talking on and on about your problems," or

- "Angry? You have a lot of nerve being angry. I should be angry about the waste of my time," or

- "Sad? Don't be so self-indulgent."

Every one of these responses is a defensive denial of John's feelings. Responses like these keep an emotionally literate dialogue from taking place. Most of the time we respond this way because we feel guilty about having hurt someone. But a defensive response can also be a way of dismissing someone we don't want to deal with.

If Mary feels misunderstood, guilty, or angry, she can talk about that later. For now what matters are John's feelings, not Mary's. It's just a matter of taking turns. What is important at this point is that Mary acknowledge what John felt when she wanted to stop talking. Then she can talk about how she feels.

Often this process calls for you to bite your tongue and be patient. Keep in mind that silence can cool down the escalation of emotionally charged conversations. But more important, it is the only fair thing to do when a friend or loved one is in emotional distress. Why? Because it gives the person a chance to get his or her distress out and gives you a chance to exercise your love and empathy.

CASE STUDY IN ACCEPTANCE

Here's an example: Marianne and Nick had decided to watch a romantic video together one evening. Nick was about to turn on the tape when Marianne stopped him.

"Hold on," she said. "I want to pour a small drink."

She went over to the liquor cabinet and poured a drink. Then she turned around and walked in a leisurely way back to the couch.

A funny TV show was on, and Marianne stood near the couch watching the set, waiting for Nick to join her so they could start their movie. Meanwhile, he had decided to put away some papers while he waited for her. He mistakenly thought she wanted to finish her drink before starting the film. He looked up and saw her laughing at the sitcom on the set, having barely touched her drink.

"When are you going to be ready?" he said with irritation.

"I've been ready," she said, surprised.

"What do you mean? I've been waiting."

"I've been right here, waiting for you."

"You haven't touched your drink."

"Yes, I have, but what does that matter?" she said, confused.

"Don't you want to finish your drink so that we can start?"

"No, I wanted to drink it during the movie."

"Fine, whatever, I just don't know what took so long," he said impatiently as he moved to turn on the movie.

This type of interaction had become a common experience between them. Marianne pressed her lips together sadly. She often felt that she took the blame for their little conflicts, and that made her very unhappy. She decided to stop this process with an action/feeling statement; she did not want to start their romantic evening feeling villified and resentful.

"Nick, I'm sorry but I need to talk to you for a few minutes before we start." He looked at her with dismay, but agreed. Marianne proceeded: "When you spoke to me just now in that tone, I felt pretty bad about it. It made me very sad."

"What was the tone?" Nick asked. He had heard this type of complaint from friends and family before.

"Well, you sounded very annoyed."

"Well, that's true, I was annoyed." He thought for a few seconds. Then he said, "I see what happened now. When I talked with you in that annoyed-sounding tone, you felt bad." He looked in Marianne eyes and asked: "Is that right?" She nodded. "I am sorry" he said, "I should work on that impatient tone of voice. Does that feel better?"

She smiled happily for a moment. "Would you kiss me?" She had been looking forward to the evening, and was very upset—hurt and fearful—by the prospect of it starting out badly.

He stopped leaning impatiently toward the VCR for the first time during their conversation, put both arms around her hips, and gave her a long kiss.

The above suggestions are designed to bring out action/feeling statements. But surely we can't speak very long without dealing with our suspicions about other people's motivations and intentions. The next step in emotionally literate dialogue is designed to deal with just that.

STEP 7

Revealing Our Intuitive Hunches

Getting a "reality check" on an intuition about another person's actions or intentions.

The use of our intuitive powers plays an absolutely central function in emotional literacy training.

Intuition is your most powerful emotional tool. With it you can make important decisions when all the facts are not available.

Before Eric Berne developed Transactional Analysis he became very interested in intuition. It was intuition, he said, that told him about the Inner Child that is behind what we do much of the time.

Most of us like to think that what we say comes from our Adult. At a party, we may act childlike and happily acknowledge it. Or, when lecturing a whiny toddler, we may be parental and make no apology for it. But in most situations, we prefer to believe we are talking to people in a logical and rational way—that is, from our Adult ego-state.

We have a hard time admitting we may be speaking irrationally, like a Child, or reacting out of prejudice, like a punitive Parent. But a great deal of what we say and do comes from ego states other than the Adult.

If we can fool ourselves about what ego state we are in, it shouldn't be surprising that we can sometimes be fooled—or at least confused—by behaviors we observe in others.

Let's take a look at a husband and wife shopping at a supermarket:

Wife (noticing a six-pack in the shopping cart): "I didn't know we were buying beer."

Is this an Adult question or an expression of Parental disapproval?

Husband (responding): "Well, yeah!"

Is this Adult confirmation to his wife's Adult question or is it Child rebelliousness?

How can you decide the ego states involved in this exchange? To do so, you have to use your intuition.

Our intuition is very useful in making an initial guess whenever we are in the dark about someone's emotions or intentions. When in doubt, scientists, detectives, and market analysts use their intuitions to guide their actions. What determines their success, however, is how accurately they check out their initial hunches. A detective who guesses the butler did it can't make the arrest without proof. A scientist who blindly follows his hunches without validating them will surely fail in the end. In the same way, if you use your intuition, you must check out your hunch before acting on it.

In the case of the shopping couple, use your intuition and ask yourself what the husband and wife dialogue sounded like. Was it Adult→Adult, or was it Parent→Child? You will probably guess right, but a guess is not good enough. Evidence must be objectively collected. It may help if you continue to observe and gather more information.

Let's listen to the wife's response.

Wife: "Oh!" (smiling) "Okay!" Her response seems to indicate that she accepts his answer as an Adult response to an Adult question.

Nothing more is said on the subject and they go about their business. Was this in fact an Adult to Adult transaction? Probably, but maybe not. If you could follow them home and be a fly on the wall, it would eventually become clear, however. Does he drink the whole six-pack before dinner? Does she throw a fit or go into a deep sulk? Or do they share a beer while they are having their hamburgers and finish the six-pack over the next two weeks?

In analyzing transactions like this, we must take care not to jump to conclusions.

Intuition is rarely completely correct or incorrect. To find out which intuitions are correct, it is necessary to check them constantly against reality.

HOW DO OTHERS FEEL?

In our daily lives we are constantly trying to understand the behavior of others. When we are not communicating well with them (which is often the case), we are forced to guess what is going on in their minds by using whatever information is available.

We don't usually ask people why they are doing whatever they are doing. We probably would not get a reliable answer even if we did ask. When we want to figure out why people do what they do we are forced to largely rely on our intuition. But using something as fuzzy as intuition doesn't always make our conclusion usable or valid. Our intuitive hunches need to be thoroughly cross-checked and modified to fit what is going on.

Because a lot of what goes on in our emotional lives tends to be dark and negative, our intuitions about people are often paranoid. This does not make them completely inaccurate, however.

These negative intuitions if left alone and not checked against reality can turn into what I call paranoid fantasies. They are fantasies because they are the product of a feverish mind, and paranoid because they are inaccurate exaggerations of a grain of truth.

I am not talking here about the kind of persecution delusions that makes paranoia a form of madness. The type of paranoia I am talking about has its origin in a heightened but distorted awareness generated by our intuition.

We are aware of many things that are never spoken about, or are discounted and denied by others. Unless we reveal our intuitions we are left guessing at the motives of those others. Unless checked out these intuitions may develop into paranoid fantasies and unspoken resentments that can ruin relationships. That is why it is important to bring our intuitions into the open and check them out.

INTUITION IN ACTION, A CASE STUDY

Jane is upset about her coworker Beth. She has been complaining to Megan about how she does not understand Beth's behavior. Beth seems spoiled to her, and she seems to have little respect for others.

Megan likes Beth and suspects that some kind of rivalry lurks behind Jane's complaints.

When Jane begins to describe how much time and attention her boss gives to Beth, Megan is sure that her guess that Jane is somehow jealous of Beth is accurate.

"It sounds as if you feel rejected by Beth, and short-changed because she gets more attention than you," says Megan.

"No, not at all," insists Jane. "Years ago I felt that way, a little. I'm just worried about her behavior, I think she's alienating a lot of people."

"But she's very well-liked," says Megan.

"I don't know how that can last, given the way she behaves," declares Jane.

"But I think the things you describe are not really that offensive, they're just assertive," says Megan. "Are you sure you don't resent something about her that's influencing your judgment?" she asks as gently as she can.

"No, no, not at all," says Jane.

Megan is stranded. Her intuition is buzzing loudly, but Jane insists she doesn't harbor any bad feelings.

The outcome is that Megan feels less and less empathy for Jane's distress. The experience of having her intuition discounted is so unpleasant that she feels unable to connect with her friend emotionally. She begins to look at her watch, longing for a change in the conversation. In this case having her intuition discounted made Megan withdraw emotionally.

When we sense something and it is denied, we have two options: Either we forget whatever it is that our intuition brought to our attention, or we persist in our idea.

If we continue to get denials and dismissals of our intuitions, our efforts to figure out what is going on may lead us far off the mark, especially if we have an active imagination.

As an example, let's go back to the ill-fated telephone call between John and Mary. When Mary abruptly terminated the telephone call, John's intuition goes into overdrive. It goes from:

- "Mary is unhappy," to

- "Mary is unhappy with me," to

- "Mary is angry with me," to

- "Mary hates me."

John begins to search for a reason for Mary to hate him. He talks to Nancy, Mary's best friend, who makes the wild guess that Mary might be put off by John's sexist attitudes.

That's it! John concludes in a final fit of paranoia: Mary hates me because she thinks I'm a sexist pig!

Meanwhile, Mary doesn't have a clue about what's going on. Although she was short with John, she was simply tired and anxious about another phone call she was expecting. She did become slightly annoyed with John, but it was not because he was being sexist. Rather, she was annoyed because he kept endlessly talking about his troubles with his friend Anne.

So John's intuition was somewhat correct, as intuitions almost always are. Mary *was* unhappy with him. When he asks if she was angry, however, her answer will likely be: "Angry? Not at all. I feel fine. I like you, John."

DISCOUNTING INTUITION

This response leaves John confused. Despite Mary's confirmation that all is well, he still has a sense that there is something wrong.

Emotionally, this is a minor catastrophe. Is he happy because Mary says she likes him? Or is he angry because she is denying that something is wrong? Does he trust her? The questions her answer generates are enough to make his head spin.

What Mary did is called an "emotional discount." It denies John's intuition that Mary is angry by dismissing it entirely. Confusion and increased paranoia are usually the result of such a response.

It is dangerous to a relationship to dismiss someone's suspicions as wholly mistaken. The other person will rightly feel that he or she cannot be totally wrong, and may begin to suspect that you are being deceitful or that you are unaware of your motives.

Here is another example of intution denied.

Donna has been having misgivings about her friendship

with Craig for a long time. Over the years she has developed a hunch that he is interested in her as more than a friend, which makes her uncomfortable. It annoys her that he always seems to have a hidden romantic agenda.

Things change when Donna meets Justin and they move in together. Suddenly Craig stops calling. Donna has come to feel so conflicted about Craig that she is almost relieved. Still, he is a dear friend and she really likes him. She doesn't want to lose him as a friend. She sends him a card with a short, friendly note enclosed, to see if he will respond. Still no phone call from Craig. So she calls him, feeling nervous. He has been depressed, he tells her, because of his continued inability to find work. She swallows hard and raises the dreaded subject: "I've been noticing that you haven't called; I was wondering if you feel uncomfortable calling me here at my new apartment with Justin."

"Oh no, not at all." Craig quickly answers, sounding sincere.

"Are you sure? Maybe you feel weird about meeting Justin for the first time over the phone?"

"No, not at all," says Craig.

Donna decides to take him at his word. But still no calls, no cards, no letters. Should she pursue him when the relationship is so fraught with unspoken friction? She decides to just leave it alone for a while.

By now Donna's mind is tangled in knots: Why would he choose to drop her as a friend now? Does he feel too humiliated to call? Is he jealous of Justin? If so, did he lie when he said he didn't feel badly about her move?

Donna feels that she has given Craig an opportunity to be honest. Instead he has negated her intuition in a baffling, deeply unpleasant way. Before long there seems to be no remnant of the friendship they had had for over four years.

The above example gives a sense of how off-putting and bewildering it can be to have one's intuition negated. On the other hand, the discovery and acknowledgment of a grain of truth in the intuition has a clarifying effect. Let's revisit the above example and see what would have happened if the truth had been found.

"Are you sure, maybe you feel weird about meeting Justin for the first time over the phone?" she asks.

This time Craig chooses to validate instead of discount Donna's intuition.

"Well, okay, since you asked, I will admit that I was a little bothered years ago when I asked to meet Justin and you said no. Then later, when you started dating him seriously, you never introduced us."

Donna is taken aback. "I thought you understood that I'm reluctant to introduce my friends to each other sometimes. I told you about how I once introduced some people who really didn't like one another, and it was pretty awkward."

True enough, but clearly there's more to be said; now it's Donna's turn to be honest.

"But, Craig, can I be honest, since you answered me honestly." She waits to get Craig's permission to proceed. "I also was nervous about introducing you to Justin because I was interested in him romantically, and I have suspected for a long time that you were interested in me. I was afraid that you would feel jealous when I started dating Justin."

Donna swallows hard. "Am I right that you have been jealous of us becoming a couple?"

Now, the moment of truth for Craig. He may deny the whole thing, or he may explain to Donna that her intuition is off, that something else was going on that she never guessed. Or he might have to admit that he feels exactly as she suspects. Perhaps he feels *both* jealous of Justin romantically *and* suspicious that she is ashamed to introduce him to her other friends.

In any case, by finding out the truth about her intuition, Donna gets an emotionally literate dialogue going. In the earlier example, Craig's complete denial leads to a stone wall of emotional information. This leaves Donna feeling bewildered and overwhelmed by Craig's unintelligible messages. After Craig's clarification of his feelings, Donna is deeply relieved and their relationship has a new chance to continue.

STEP 8

Validating an Intuitive Hunch

A search for the truth—no matter how small—that can be found in an intuition.

Most of us have defensive tendencies that prevent us from admitting that another person's intuitions are true. We might consider such an admission a sign of weakness on our part, or we may be reluctant to hurt another person's feelings. In any event, the person who is presented with another's intuition must overcome his reluctance and pursue its validation, if an emotionally literate dialogue is to result.

Let's return to John and Mary. Mary has just discounted John's suspicion that she hung up on him because she was angry by saying: "Angry? Not at all. I feel fine. I like you, John."

John insists: "Somehow I thought something was amiss. Am I wrong?"

Mary thinks. She knows that she should try to find some grain of truth in his suspicions. "Actually, John, I was angry after you called, not at you, but at Nancy—maybe that's it."

Still, John may feel that this does not explain his feelings. In that case, he should pursue the matter further.

"Well, that doesn't deal with my feeling that you were angry with me, especially. Was there something wrong while we were talking?"

This might cause Mary to consider just exactly why she sounded irritated and decided to terminate the telephone conversation. After all, John does have a habit of going on and on over the telephone. Plus, she did not really want to talk about his failed friendship with Anne anymore. Since he seems willing to hear her criticism, maybe she could risk being honest. She tries.

"Actually, I was not really angry at you, but when you called I was tired and expecting another call. I was slightly irritated that you talked so long about what you wanted to discuss. I thought I was giving you hints that I didn't want to talk about Anne anymore, but you didn't seem to catch on. Does that make sense?"

Though slightly embarrassed to learn that he has been a bore, John is relieved by Mary's explanation. Something *was* wrong. But Mary was not angry at him, only irritated. Now he knows what the problem was. He understands his and her feelings at the time and where they came from. He realizes he has tried her patience going on and on about Anne. He can now believe that she likes him after all.

The facts that Mary has stipulated and John's intuitive feelings now fit together like a jigsaw puzzle. He may feel embarrassed at having bored Mary, but his awful fear that Mary hates him is laid to rest. He feels okay; he has been validated.

Sometimes the entire intuition will be correct, not just part of it. For example, this conversation could easily have confirmed John's entire intuition. It could have gone like this:

"Yes, John, I am angry with you. In fact, I've been really disappointed in you lately. I'm not sure I want to go on being friends. I've been wondering when you would get the hint and stop calling me."

Harsh words indeed, and not very emotionally literate, but better for John to hear them clearly expressed than to have to live in a confusing and endlessly hurtful emotional climate. John and Mary may go on to explore why she doesn't like him anymore, his tendency to talk on and on, and her inability to be clear when she doesn't want to talk. Or they may drop the matter, and the friendship. Either way, they are several steps ahead in the process of understanding each other and living emotionally literate lives.

Usually, however, matters are not nearly so far gone. Most problems of this sort are solvable, and when that is the case, this type of dialogue works wonders to repair the little misunderstand-ings that otherwise erode a relationship.

FRANK COMMUNICATION

Being able to discuss each other's feelings can bring spectacular results, especially when both people are committed to frank, cooperative communication.

In emotional literacy training workshops, I explain how in-tuition, when used in an effective and emotionally literate way, can greatly help us understand one another.

For example, Sarah and Julie were attending one of my work-shops. Julie is 27 years old, with a model-like figure. She is con-sidered very beautiful, even though she dresses down in order not to attract attention. Sarah is 35 and having problems keeping her weight down. They are office mates who have been having some unpleasant arguments. Julie is upset and has actually been feeling afraid of coming to work because of these disputes.

In the midst of a discussion about intuition, Julie asked Sarah if she could talk to her about a hunch that she had.

"I have a suspicion that you think that I'm stupid," Julie said with great trepidation. "I also suspect that you think I am incompetent and willing to submit to anything that the admin-istration dishes out. Is that true?"

Sarah shook her head and anxiously responded: "Not at all. I think you're very smart."

Julie slumped in her chair, discouraged. At this point I ex-plained that there is usually some truth in people's hunches. Rather than flatly denying Julie's hunch, it might be better for Sarah to think about what—if anything—may be true in Julie's fantasy.

"Emotional Literacy involves honoring other people's in-tuition, rather than discounting it," I reminded the group. "You have to be willing to look deeply into your own motives."

I let that thought soak in for a moment and then asked Sarah if there was any truth to Julie's intuition.

Sarah thought for several seconds and then nodded. "Julie, I guess your hunch is correct, in a way," she said nervously. "I do think that you're very smart, but I'm angry at you because I believe that you scare easily and go along with people who intimidate you. That makes me think you're weak. But I do believe you're very smart."

Julie felt better at hearing Sarah's true feelings, and was able to agree that she was too easily intimidated and longed to learn to stand her ground. Then she revealed another of her intuitions: "I have another hunch, and this one is scary to bring up, but we agreed to be honest, so I feel I should. Do you want to hear what I am thinking?"

"OK," Sarah said with a worried expression.

"Well," said Julie, "I also am guessing that you resent that I'm younger and that the men around the office find me attractive. I worry that you seem to believe that I am some kind of bimbo."

Everyone in the workshop became very quiet, nervously looking at Sarah and wondering how she would respond. I have to admit I was nervous, too. Regardless of the number of workshops I have led, I always feel a certain nervousness when one of the participants brings up a scary subject like this.

"This is not easy but I have to agree that I am jealous of the attention you get from the men around here," admitted Sarah. "That is part of my anger. I am not proud of that, but it's true."

The group fell silent, as everyone wrestled with the awkwardness that they felt. Another group member named Mark finally broke the ice with a question. Eventually, Sarah and Julie got several heartfelt strokes for their courage and honesty.

The group went on and on, exploring the subtleties of relationships in the office. After a two day workshop the group members left feeling empowered and optimistic.

As you can see, when we follow Opening the Heart with these two techniques—the Action/Feeling Statement and Validating an Intuitive Hunch—an emotionally literate dialogue ensues, in which suspicion, fear, recrimination, and guilt are avoided.

Through these dialogues, people learn to speak honestly and gather information about how they feel about each other. They discover how their actions affect one another's feelings, and how their intuitions reflect and distort reality. They do this without judgments, accusations, or emotional chaos, while working toward the possibility of trust.

EMPATHY MATURES

In a relationship, as trust and frank communication develop, people routinely share their intuitive hunches and will find the grain of truth to validate other's intuitions. This ongoing dialogue fine tunes people's understanding of each others' emotional terrain. People learn how others are likely to feel in certain situations and what puts them at ease. With these transactions, practiced over time, intuition matures into a powerful empathetic sense. Intuition often starts as a vague understanding that we are barely aware of, and becomes a powerful searchlight illuminating the emotional landscape and rendering it familiar and accessible. This heart-centered capacity to feel with others is an essential component of the next stage of the training: Taking Responsibility.

CASE STUDY

Putting It All Together

Now let's see how it works when we put together the steps we have covered so far.

Carter and Sandra work with each other. Sandra, the owner of the company, is Carter's boss. About six months ago they became involved in a sexual relationship. Now, after months of romantic bliss, they have begun to argue. They have asked me as a friend to help them disentangle the conflicts and bad feelings that are plaguing them.

I like both of them and worry that they have created an impossible muddle for themselves. My fear is that they will either have to stop working together or break up, or both. They want to see if they can keep their working rapport while preserving their romantic relationship. Despite their recent difficulties, they both say they have strong feelings for each other and would like to forge a long-term commitment.

Their fights began at work with arguments over business policy and customer relations. Carter is friendly and easygoing with clients, while Sandra tends to be more cut and dried. This is usually a good balance, except that Carter has given credit to three clients who aren't paying their bills. Sandra wants him to demand immediate payment, which he refuses to do. Both think the other is being unreasonable. Sandra feels that Carter is putting a strain on the company's finances, while Carter thinks that Sandra's attitude is going to alienate their clients.

This conflict at work has spilled over into their private life. They seem to disagree about everything now. Their sexual relationship has all but ceased and the honeymoon appears to be over.

After several phone conversations, I invite them to dinner to talk things over. After dessert, I suggest we begin the discussion. Sandra seems sad and Carter appears to be angry, but neither speaks of how he or she feels. Instead, they criticize each other. Sandra complains that Carter used to be passionate and is now sexually lazy. Carter says that he feels constantly nagged and criticized and sexually used.

After listening for a while I interject. "Listen, it's pretty clear that you are both upset. Don't you agree?"

Sandra nods. Carter, stone-faced, seems willing to hear me out.

"I would like to help you both clarify why you are so upset, and to do that I suggest that we use what I call the action/feeling technique. Are you willing to try?"

They both nod.

"It's very simple. You take turns filling in the blanks in an action/feeling statement, such as: When you (action), I felt (emotion). The goal is to describe a specific action and the emotion (or emotions) that resulted. No frills, just those two facts: An action and the consequent feelings.

"Anyone want to start?" I asked. "Trust me, it will be interesting. The point is to get an idea of each other's emotional landscape and to explore what is going on between you.

"Before we start, one more thing." I explained how important it was to ask for permission every time something emotionally loaded is said.

After an uncomfortable minute, Sandra took the lead.

"Can I tell you something I felt last night?" she asked Carter. After he agreed, she continued.

"When you disappointed me last night, I felt you did not love me anymore."

"Whoa, Sandra, hold on!" I interrupted. "It will take some work to turn that into an action/feeling statement. Can I try?" Sandra nodded. "You say he disappointed you. That's not a clear-cut action. What did he do?"

"After leading me on all evening, he rolled over and went to sleep as soon as we went to bed," said Sandra. "That was very disappointing and I felt he was no longer in love with me."

"What we are after here is a simple statement of emotions following actual behavior," I said. "First, let's agree that he went to sleep."

I looked over to Carter and saw that he did not dispute Sandra's statement. Turning to Sandra, I asked: "What exactly did you feel when he went to sleep? Let's talk in terms of primary emotions such as sad, mad, or ashamed."

"All three," she shot back.

"Well, which was first and how strong?" I asked.

"Shame. I was ashamed of how sexually needy I was then very sad, and now I'm angry, very angry." Tears welled up in her eyes.

"Okay, now I'll make an action/feeling statement out of the information you've given me, cutting out the accusations. 'Last night when you fell asleep instead of making love to me, I felt ashamed, very sad, and then angry.' You see?" Sandra nodded, drying her eyes.

Carter sat quietly with a blank expression. I turned to him. "Do you follow that, Carter?"

"Yeah, but I didn't really—"

"I'm sure that you have a lot to say about this situation," I interrupted. "But right now I just want you to tell me whether you understand what Sandra said. Namely, that she was ashamed, sad, and angry because you fell asleep as soon as you went to bed last night. It'll help clarify what's going on between you."

"Okay, I can see that. Can I say how *I* feel?"

"By all means."

"I feel that I have become Sandra's whipping boy. She criticizes me, and then she wants me to make passionate love to her. I can't do what she wants me to do at work or in bed, and I feel pushed around."

Again, I explained the problem with "feeling pushed around" being a non-feeling, and the need for a succinct statement relating actions to feelings. Eventually Carter pinpointed several occasions in which Sandra made critical statements. Then he was able to articulate the feelings that he experienced: "Anger, sadness."

They went back and forth. Sandra spoke of Carter's easy-going financial approach and how it scared her, while Carter addressed his feelings of embarrassment when he had to accept that Sandra owned the business and received a better education than he did.

Throughout this discussion I deflected the suspicious intuitions they had about each other. Sandra's fear was that Carter did not love her anymore and was only with her because of the job. Carter was suspicious that the only thing Sandra appreciated about him was his sexuality. Once they had both discussed those fears and resentments and expressed simple feelings without inferring motives, we were ready to move on to validating each other's intuitive hunches.

ENTER INTUITION

Though I encouraged them both to speak only about primary emotional states—feeling sad, ashamed, guilty, angry—more complicated emotional reactions kept coming up. In only about one hour we had already gotten a lot of information out: Sandra's belief that she was being sexually teased and the fear that Carter no longer loved her, and Carter's belief that Sandra was critical of his lack of education and saw him as a sexual servant.

Then we moved on. I explained to them that complicated emotional reactions like these consist of simple, primary emotions that lead to negative intuitions. I told them that we were now ready to deal with these speculations, and asked each of them to state their suspicions, which I had before asked them to censor.

I had just one rule, however: Listen to each other with an open mind. Instead of denying one another's accusations, look for the truth in them, however small.

I started off with a question: Did Sandra think of Carter as merely a sexy man without any brains? This was one of Carter's fears, which she categorically denied. Still I invited her to think it over.

"Sandra, let's assume that Carter isn't crazy and that if he believes these things, then there may be some truth to them," I said. "It does no good to discount what he experiences. Instead, why don't you think of what truth there may be in his fears, however small."

Her brow furrowed as she fell silent. Eventually she spoke.

"It is true that I appreciate the way you make love to me, Carter. And it is also true that I want that kind of response from you as much as anything else that you give me. And I do think that when we make love you are wonderfully mindless. But I think you are right, that feeling becomes part of the way I see you all the time and that could be hurtful to you."

"It is," said Carter.

After a few moments of uncomfortable silence, Sandra asked Carter, "Can I tell you something I am afraid you think about me?"

He agreed to hear what she had to say.

"This is very hard to say, but I'm afraid you think I'm frigid."

"Sexually you mean?" he asked.

"Yes," said Sandra on the verge of tears.

He thought for a long time. Then he looked at me with puzzled confusion.

"Think about it," I said. "Why would she get that impression? Do you think she is cold in some way?"

"Well, yeah, I think she is cold sometimes," he said, turning to Sandra. "The way you want to treat the customers is cold, in a way. And sometimes you treat me that way, too. I have thought that. But in bed you're passionate when you want to be, or maybe I should say when you feel good about me."

Sandra agreed. "I guess that must have been what I was picking up, that you think I am cold in the way I deal with business. I hate that part of me," she said, again starting to cry.

Carter moved over and hugged her. "I don't hate it, I admire it. I admire the way you take care of business. Just don't close my account."

They both laughed.

The conversation went on as we continued to map the feelings that they both had.

We looked at how they had been busy drawing destructive conclusions from each other's actions, creating bad feelings in both of them.

I pointed out how relationships have a tendency to fall into channels or ruts that can take two possible directions, positive or negative. Love, mutual consideration, trust, kindness, sexual abandon, and personal admiration can feed upon each other to create a good relationship just as anger, selfishness, resentment, and negative judgments feed on one another to ruin it.

Sandra and Carter's relationship had shifted from a positive state—the honeymoon period of increasing affection and passion—to a negative one. It would take energy and effort to reinstate the positive cycle and eventually settle into it, but now they knew what they felt, how strongly, and why, and that would certainly help.

Sandra and Carter went on to couple's therapy and continued their emotional education. To this date they seem to be doing well and claim that our after-dinner conversation was the beginning of their renewed relationship.

S U M M A R Y

Surveying the Emotional Landscape

Despite what the pop psychologists would have you believe, you *can* cause emotions in another person and vice versa. That's why the action/feeling statement is so valuable. You can use it to clarify the feelings that are caused by your and other people's actions without making accusations or being judgmental.

The format is simple: "When you (action), I felt (emotion)."

If you correctly use action/feeling statements, you will over a period of time begin to shed light upon the emotional landscape that surrounds you. You will have a tool to learn how people feel, how strongly, and why and how these feelings relate to other people's actions.

Learning to hear and understand how we affect other people's feelings with our actions, without becoming defensive, is very important in this process. As you improve your Emotional Literacy, you will be able to sense other people's emotions using your intuition. You will learn to state your intuitive hunches to people and as the truth in these hunches is validated through feedback your intuition will mature into an empathic sense. This loving empathic sense is the foundation of emotionally literate behavior. With it we can confront difficult emotional situations head on and prevent them from escalating as we unlock the door to richer, more rewarding relationships.

6

STAGE THREE

TAKING RESPONSIBILITY

The most difficult and final step in learning Emotional Literacy is taking responsibility for the mistakes we make in our relationships.

If most of us look at our lives honestly, we will be able to see just how human we truly are, and how many mistakes we have made.

We know that we make mistakes all the time. We hurt the people we love, we lie to our friends, we betray people who trust us, we try to help and then when we fail and they seem unwilling to be helped, we persecute people who need us. When we make these mistakes and we realize them, we blame ourselves or we blame our victims or we make empty apologies. None of these solutions works very well. It is much better to understand why we keep repeating these errors and then take steps to correct them.

Eric Berne, with his theory of games and scripts, gaves us a very effective way to understand why we make the emotional mistakes we make. Let me explain.

THE GAMES PEOPLE PLAY

If you follow people around and watch their conversations, you'll notice that some people have the same unpleasant transaction over and over. Some people get mean and wind up scaring others. Some people turn every conversation into a joke. Others always make anyone they talk with depressed. Most of us have one such pattern, sometimes more than one, that we repeat over and over. When we do this, we are playing a game.

Pay attention and notice the feelings that result from these conversations. In conversations where people play games, one or more people wind up feeling bad—sad, angry, scared, and so on. Other conversations go smoothly and seem to make people feel good. They are probably free of games. Either way, people are getting strokes. When people play games they exchange negative strokes. When conversations are free of games, the transactions are positive and the strokes are good.

Berne discovered that there are different kinds of games. For instance, some people play depressing games like "Kick Me," others play angry games like "Now I've Got You," and yet others play self-destructive games like "Alcoholism."

Why do people play games?

There are different theories. One of them is that people playing a game are making a misguided attempt to get positive strokes, an attempt that backfires, producing negative strokes instead.

I agree with this theory and have come to the conclusion that people play games because they are starved for strokes and will get them at any cost, even if all they get is bad strokes.

Scripts: Decisions That Rule Our Lives. Though games are failed, hurtful attempts to get positive strokes, every completed game gives the player a payoff: It confirms a certain view of the world that the player has chosen to adopt. This enables the game player to see his life as coherent and intelligible, even though his worldview is negative.

Some typically negative worldviews are "Nice guys always get the shaft," or "Never trust a woman (man)," or "Mess with me and you'll regret it." Such a view, though negative, gives the player a sense that he understands the world, rotten though it is.

Early in life, people decide on their life expectations. These decisions become blueprints for living, or scripts, similar to the scripts of movies or plays. Many people read their lines from these scripts for the rest of their lives.

Every time a person plays a game to its conclusion, he or she gets a feeling of bittersweet satisfaction called the "script (or existential) payoff." This feeling tells her that even though she is all messed up, at least she knows who she is and what the meaning of her life really is.

Some very bad existential statements that nevertheless give meaning to life are "Born to lose," "Everybody hates me," "Nothing ever works out." At the end of a terrible day, we can at least say to ourselves, "I knew it. Life is hell and then you die." At the end of a terrible life we can say, "Yep. Just as I thought. Life was hell and now I'm dying."

Games are part of these total life patterns or scripts. The "Why don't you?" "Yes, but . . ." player has a depressive script; the "Kick Me" player has a victim script; the angry player has a persecutor script; the Alcoholic has a tragic, self-destructive script, and so on.

One kind of script decision we make early in life deals with our emotions. Often we head for one emotional extreme or its opposite. Neither of them leads to Emotional Literacy or a fulfilling life.

We decide to cut off our feelings and wind up permanently numb, or we decide to be intensely emotional and not control our feelings, and we wind up living in emotional chaos. We decide not to love and become hard and cold; or we decide to love all the way and wind up constantly disappointed. We decide to avoid anger at all costs and become totally passive, or we decide to express anger freely and become violent. We decide to stop feeling or we decide to go with every feeling we have.

But decisions like these eventually lead us into emotional

dead ends. And because the script that leads us there is so much a part of us, we have a hard time seeing what is going on. To get out of this fix, however, we have to look at the major patterns of our lives. Anyone who finds himself regularly in trouble with people will, upon reflection, probably see he is caught in a series of games that form a life script decided early in life due to an unhappy or traumatic event at the time.

Take the worker who regularly gets fired. Or the woman who gets dumped by her lovers over and over again. Or the man who repeatedly gets drunk. If you are always late, always in debt, always forgetting things, always lying to cover your mistakes, or always getting taken for your last penny, chances are these endless mishaps are part of a lifelong script.

There are many theories that try to explain why our lives get as messed up as they do, why we get so depressed that we lose interest in life, why we go crazy, or why we become addicts or hurt people around us. Most of these theories blame our parents. Some theories blame our parents' genes, saying these troubles are hereditary. Others blame our parents' behavior, claiming they mistreated us and taught us to be depressed, crazy, or drunk. All of these theories are somewhat true for some people and very true for others. There are hereditary aspects to alcoholism, madness, and depression. Some of us do learn from our parents to be depressed, dishonest, or angry, or to act crazy or to get high. Finally, some of us have had difficult childhoods that have left us confused and frightened.

Still, even if there is something in our genes that makes us act as we do, and even though our childhood experiences may have damaged us badly, life is still made up of daily experiences that are shaped by our daily decisions and behavior.

If we change those experiences by changing our decisions and behaviors and by rectifying our mistakes, our life can be changed as well.

We can change the patterns of our lives by deciding to change our scripts and by finding meaning in a different kind of life plan, in which we are good to other people instead of hurting them. This is a decision in favor of Emotional Literacy and has a transformative effect on those around us as well as ourselves.

Rescuer, Persecutor, and Victim. How do we break out of these emotional traps? Since scripts are not hardwired into our brains, since they are based on our own decisions, we are not stuck with them. We can change them by changing our minds and acting in new, more productive ways.

The first requirement to change our scripts is to understand the three main destructive roles that people play in their games. These roles are the Rescuer, the Persecutor, and the Victim. They are common to all games. When we are acting out an old script, we select one of the three roles to play.

Rescuers take care of people who should take care of themselves, letting them off the hook, preventing them from making their own decisions or from finding their own way. Persecutors criticize, preach, and punish. Victims are incapable of making decisions, letting others run their lives and take care of them.

Why do we stick to these roles? Because we have learned to get strokes by playing them, and because the roles give meaning to our lives.

It's curious but true that everyone who plays one of these roles eventually switches over and plays the two others also.

That's why, in Transactional Analysis, as suggested by Stephen Karpman (see References) we arrange these three roles in a triangle to show how people move from one role to the other in an endless merry-go-round.

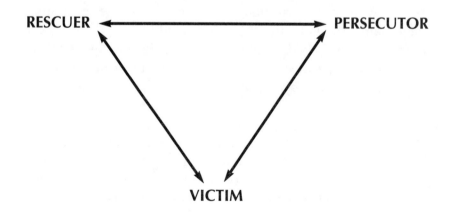

In fact, these roles are so important to us that each of them has been legitimized by becoming the basis for a political ideology. The Persecutor has been adopted by conservative extremists who want to abandon all responsibility for their fellow humans and would jail and disown every person who fails to be a "good" citizen. The Rescuer role is the pet attitude of "tax-and-spend" liberals who would sacrifice all our resources taking care of other people. The Victim is the preferred role for any group whose members are embattled against society or unwilling to take care of themselves and who would prefer to be taken care of by others.

Now, this doesn't mean that these attitudes aren't sometimes legitimate. It can be laudable to take care of other people. It can be fine to demand that people take care of themselves. It is reasonable to demand help when we are unable to go on. But when any of these approaches hardens into a political dogma that can't be challenged, or an inflexible role, it becomes harmful and unproductive.

How do you tear up your scripts, stop the games, and reclaim your life? The answer is that you have to give up the roles of Rescuer, Persecutor, and Victim.

But we have to be careful when we do that to make sure that we are not just jumping from one role to another. It is very important to realize that if you play one role you will eventually play the other two. When a person tries to stop playing games, his first tendency is to move to a different role in the same game. If you are the Victim in a game of Alcoholism (that is, the alcoholic), you may think you are changing by switching to the Persecutor or Rescuer role. You may believe you are changing, but that is not an improvement. It is merely the same game with a rearranged cast.

CASE STUDY

Role Switching

Harry is an alcoholic. He drinks every day and gets drunk every weekend. His wife Helen drinks moderately but is a chain smoker. After one particularly nasty weekend binge and Monday morning hangover, Harry decides to stop drinking. On Wednesday he still hasn't had a drink and he feels squeaky clean and self-righteous. He starts persecuting Helen for smoking, while he tries to persuade her that she is also an alcoholic and should give up drinking altogether.

She has been through all this before. She is unimpressed by his arguments and angry that he is harassing her. He feels that he has changed. She knows he hasn't. She tells him to get off her back and go to an Alcoholics Anonymous meeting. He says he doesn't need AA.

To make a long story short, by Friday Harry is drinking again and blaming Helen's attitude for his relapse.

That's the story of a Alcoholic game player who didn't change. Let's take a look at a Rescuer who fails to escape her script even though she thinks she is doing so by adopting the role of Persecutor.

Helen has been rescuing Harry for years. One day she reads about codependency and decides to cut Harry off completely. She smashes all the liquor bottles in the house, changes the lock of the front door, and tells Harry that he can't come into the house if he is drinking. When Harry gets home from work after a few drinks at the bar, she refuses to let him in and calls the cops when he starts banging at the door. When the cops arrive she lets Harry back in, the cops leave, and Harry knocks her around, switching from Victim to Persecutor. They are back where they started. Again this is an extreme, inflexible approach to the problem and represents no real change.

Obviously, these are not real solutions. If you are caught in a script like this, what you need to do is to face yourself and your actions honestly, admit that you may have been wrong, and admit that you need help, including new and better ideas. You need to jump off the role-playing merry-go-round altogether. You need to start getting your strokes honestly, instead of having to play games to get them.

This is easier said than done, but it can be done. Berne believed that most of us are basically okay and that, given a chance, we can find happiness and live mentally healthy lives. Hence, the famous saying, "I'm OK, you're OK." To make this change, each person needs to find the "OK core" in him- or herself and recognize it in the next person.

There is no better way to find your OK core than to resolve to act differently from this moment on; to love and take care of yourself at the same time that you love and take care of others. In other words, not to Rescue, not to Persecute and not to be a Victim. And nothing will remind us of our previous mistakes better than making a heartfelt apology and amends for them. This is why this last part of the program teaches you to apologize and make amends.

THE IMPORTANCE OF TAKING RESPONSIBILITY

The mistakes we make, often swept under the rug, have a cumulative, lasting, and corrosive effect on our relationships. After years of accumulated emotional damage, many relationships become cold and distant or simply end.

To bring about real and lasting change in a relationship that has been allowed to devolve owing to emotional errors, we have to take responsibility. After all, we can become receptive to relationships by opening our hearts, and we can learn the terrain of the emotional landscape, but emotional damage cannot be fixed between people without an effort to define and admit the faults and errors committed.

The problem is that very few people are emotionally skilled enough to apologize sincerely and nondefensively. In short, most people don't know how to say they are sorry.

The final emotional literacy skill I teach concerns the fine art of acknowledging one's mistakes and asking, even begging, for forgiveness.

The thought of making a deeply felt apology strikes terror in the heart of the average person. Losing face, backing off, eating crow—all bring back memories of humiliating schoolyard struggles. We have learned to believe that backing down is weak and humiliating. Yet an emotionally mature person will admit mistakes and apologize for any harm caused by his or her actions.

I can use an example from my own life to illustrate this point.

Personal Case in Point. I had just arrived in Chicago from Europe and went immediately to a hotel, where I had made reservations. I was exhausted by the flight and ready for a hot bath and a long night's sleep. The clerk, a gentle young woman, looked at her book and after some searching politely shook her head.

"I'm sorry, Dr. Steiner, but we have no reservation for you today. Your reservation is for tomorrow and we have no rooms tonight."

I was outraged by this news.

"But I specifically called weeks ago . . ."

"Yes, and I see here that we listed you for tomorrow," she insisted.

"Well, that was your mistake!" I barked.

As I carried on loudly I began to realize in the back of my mind that I was wrong. I had assumed that the reservation would be for the day after I left France, but had forgotten that I would in fact arrive the same day on an east-to-west flight from Europe to the United States. Meanwhile, the clerk had called someone on the phone and was explaining the situation.

After a minute she hung up and said, "Dr. Steiner, we will try to get you a room, but . . ."

At that point I wasn't listening. I had been teaching Emotional Literacy in Europe, and I knew that I had to practice what

I preached, even if it meant the possibility of ending up on the street.

"Can I apologize to you?" I asked, my face flushed with embarrassment.

She looked up, puzzled.

"I just realized that you were right," I continued. "When I called to make my reservation, I was assuming that I would arrive the day after my departure from Paris."

"That's okay," she said. "This happens all the time, people don't realize that there is no time difference when they come back. But people never apologize."

"Well, I owe you an apology for the way I spoke to you before," I insisted. "Will you accept it?"

"Oh, That's all right," she said looking back down at her book.

"No, no, seriously, will you accept my apology?"

She looked at me and smiled. "Sure, why not? I really appreciate it," she said. "People expect us to apologize for our mistakes but rarely apologize for theirs."

As you might guess, this story has a happy ending. She found a room for me and before long I was comfortably asleep. I had practiced what I preached and felt great because of it. I had a room and had enjoyed a refreshingly honest interaction with a gracious young woman, all because of a mistake.

There are a number of obstacles that must be overcome before we can take responsibility and make a heartfelt apology.

1. Admitting to ourselves that we have made a mistake: Deciding that we have made a mistake is very difficult for most of us because we then become vulnerable to harsh criticism from our Critical Parent.

Typical of the criticism you might hear in your mind are some of the following:

- "You fool, what a stupid mistake to make, and then you had to make an even worse fool of yourself by getting into an argument."

- "Right, as usual you simply don't know better." or

- "You have always been crazy, see what you have done now!"

Remember, the goal of the Critical Parent is to make you feel inadequate and not okay, and when you admit a mistake to yourself you give your Critical Parent a perfect opportunity to do just that.

2. Admitting our mistake to others: As if admitting mistakes to ourselves is not enough, admitting to someone else that we have made a mistake makes us vulnerable to their anger and disappointment as well as the further scrutiny and wrath of our Critical Parent.

This can be a big, humiliating obstacle, but one we must learn to overcome. Admitting our mistakes is a powerful, cleansing experience, one that everyone with any claims to Emotional Literacy needs to experience.

3. Feeling and conveying true regret: This is where having an open heart will be indispensable, for even if we know and admit to a mistake we have made, we don't necessarily recognize or regret the damage we may have caused. That is why this phase of Emotional Literacy comes last: It is hard to apologize for emotional damage we don't understand.

Empathy has to be developed before we can recognize the pain that we cause others with our actions. Without that recognition, it is hard to assume responsibility. Through the empathy developed in this work, we can see how our actions may have made another person feel sad, ashamed, angry, or afraid. Only when we *really* see that will we be inclined to regret our actions.

4. Finally, admitting that amends are needed: Taking responsibility for a mistake usually means making amends. Amends means changing our behavior and even making reparations. When we make amends we no longer do the things that have hurt others. We stop playing the role we have played in the past.

Making amends is an important aspect of obtaining forgiveness. By making amends, we put our money where our mouths are, as it were, and in many cases forgiveness would not be possible without them.

By following the advice presented here in Stage Three, you will understand what it means to take responsibility for your actions. You will learn how to admit—to yourself as well as the victim(s) of your mistake—that you have done something wrong and that you wish to do what is necessary to set things right.

Remember, we all make mistakes, including emotional ones. By becoming Emotionally Literate, we learn to avoid mistakes from the beginning and to rectify those we make as quickly as possible.

HOW PLAYING THE RESCUER, PERSECUTOR, AND VICTIM LEAD TO COMMON EMOTIONAL MISTAKES

We have already discussed the three emotionally destructive roles people play in their everyday lives. Now let's look at these rules in more detail.

The Rescuer. A Rescue is a transactional event, part of a very common form of behavior known also as "codependence" or "enabling." It usually begins with an excessive willingness to be helpful that later causes problems and conflict. We play the Rescuer when we do things for other people that we don't want to do, or when we do more than our share.

We are inspired to rescue people when they seem to be unable to take responsibility for themselves.

Some people are habitual Rescuers and will rescue others at the slightest provocation, even if the other person has no real desire to be rescued. When we do this it is usually because:

1. We like to feel needed.

2. We mistake competent people who are having difficulties for helpless people who are having difficulties.

3. We were raised to feel we always have to make people happy.

Ellen is a habitual Rescuer.

She learns that her long-time neighbor Richard has AIDS. The next time she sees Richard, she feels compelled to be very thoughtful, and to allude to his illness only with the utmost tact and concern.

Eventually, the strain of working to make Richard feel good makes it unpleasant for her even to see him. Ellen is vaguely aware that Richard is an extremely self-sufficient and spiritually balanced man who doesn't really need her intense emotional output. However, Rescuing is such a deeply ingrained habit that she doesn't know how to stop.

This Rescue makes Ellen's dealings with Richard exhausting, to the point that she begins to avoid him. Still, in the back of her mind, she knows she is making a bad situation worse for Richard and feels guilty for drawing Richard into her Rescue game. This situation is typical for Ellen, who is constantly trying to do good for others but often is creating rather than solving problems for people.

Rescues can also stem from a subtle desire to make others indebted to us, or an inability to say no when something is asked of us. In any case, we Rescue when we either:

- Do something we don't want to do, or

- Do more than our share in a situation.

It is very important to distinguish rescuing as a humanitarian activity from Rescuing as an emotionally damaging role.

That is why in Transactional Analysis we write them in lower case and capitals respectively.

Clearly if someone is helpless and needs food, medical attention, or solace, we can be of help and should do so. If we come in at a crucial moment and literally save someone's life, we have rescued him or her in a profoundly positive way. Very often, however, in cases when we are "helping" others, we are actually causing harm, even though we probably feel that we are doing good.

A person who is a habitual Rescuer, always doing more than her share and engaging in activities that she doesn't really want to participate in, is most likely creating interpersonal problems. Unwanted Rescuing fosters selfishness, dependence, and helpless behavior on the part of the Rescued/Victim. It also takes away the Rescued person's initiative and personal power, while it eventually creates anger and resentment in both the Rescuer and the Rescued.

The Persecutor. Again one characteristic of these three roles is that if you play one, you will eventually play the other two. For instance, it is inevitable that Rescuers will eventually become overwhelmed by the needs of those they are Rescuing.

They will become tired of taking care of others, and develop a hatred of those they have Rescued for needing and taking so much. Even though the Rescuer made the initial mistake, he will not become angry at himself but at those to whom so much has been given. After all, "Didn't I give everything and get nothing in return?"

At this point Rescuers become Persecutors of their Victims.

Peter is a talented machinist and substance abuser. After work he usually goes directly to the bar and has a couple of beers. When he gets home he is slightly drunk and plops himself in front of the TV hoping that Jacquie, his wife, will come home and fix something to eat.

Jacquie works, too. When she gets home she usually cooks something, even though she knows that Peter will not be willing to do the dishes.

Still, she cooks and eventually cleans up, thinking that Peter's job is very stressful and that she should not nag him. By the time they go to bed, Peter is extremely high from a couple of extra beers. They haven't had sex in years.

Peter and Jacquie's finances are also stressed from overspending on eating out and legal fees from Peter's drunk-driving conviction.

After a couple of years of this, Jacquie has finally had enough. She meets a nice, sober man at work and has sex with him, in part to get even with Peter. She likes this new man and a couple of months later during a fight over the dishes Jacquie announces to Peter that she is leaving him.

Jacquie has abruptly switched from being the Rescuer to being the Persecutor.

Peter is stunned and feels totally victimized. He cries and begs and claims not to understand. He goes to the bar and talks to the bartender. He listens to Country-Western songs about the cruelty of women. He is now a full-fledged "helpless" Victim.

Fortified by some bad advice and liquor he decides to go home and take command of the situation. He smashes through the locked door and threatens Jacquie. Peter has switched from Victim to Persecutor and Jacquie has now switched from Rescuer to sudden Persecutor to terrorized Victim.

She goes to stay with her mother, who sides with Peter. As a result, Jacquie spends a week in abject depression and insecurity, blaming herself for the entire problem.

Eventually she talks to a counselor who takes her side. She switches from Victim to Persecutor again. She files a restraining order against Peter and gets a divorce lawyer. He switches from Persecutor to Victim, apologizes and begs her to forgive him. Going from Persecutor to Rescuer, she feels sorry for him and agrees to move back home with him. Within a week Peter is drinking again and the process repeats itself, only this time Peter actually strikes Jacquie.

They go round the Rescue-Persecutor-Victim merry-go-round for a few more years until Peter meets another woman who does not mind his drinking and finds him charming.

Jacquie is stunned by the reversal. Without some help or intervention, they both will continue to play these games with their family and friends, possibly until they die.

Jacquie needs to stop this process and refuse to Rescue, Persecute, or be Victimized. Instead of abruptly switching from Rescuer to Persecutor, she should get support from friends or a self-help group like Al-Anon, then develop a plan of action that takes care of her needs and helps Peter decide what he will do to take care of his. Then she should apologize to Peter for Rescuing him, and promise not to anymore. After all this is accomplished she may feel that the relationship does not work and may decide to leave Peter. If she does that however it will not be a role-switch but a genuine script change. An example of how to do this follows later in this chapter.

The Victim. As we have just seen, when people rescue they eventually get angry. When this happens the recipient of the Rescuer's misguided generosity will become aware of the Rescuer's anger and contempt. The Rescued/Victim will begin to feel demeaned, treated like a charity case.

Few people enjoy being viewed as a Victim, which is why, when people realize they are being rescued, they feel humiliated and resentful.

The above example is a real-life example of the Rescue cycle. Eric Berne used to talk of first-, second-, and third-degree game playing. You can tell the severity of these roles from the harm eventually done to the Victim.

If the Victim is physically abused, as in the case of Jacquie, we have a case of third-degree Rescue and Persecution. In more common first-degree cases, the harm to the Victim is in the area of humiliation, hurt, and sadness. Third-degree game playing ends up in suicide or mayhem.

Now we come to the touchy subject of the Victim's role and his or her responsibility for what is happening.

Clearly some people are overwhelmed by other people's single-minded purpose to persecute them. An example would be the Jews in World War II, blacks in inner cities, or rape and incest victims. Yet in some cases, the Victim contributes to the situation by accepting it. Certainly in the case of Jacquie, she has been cooperating with what is happening to her.

There is a tendency to blame women who are victims of spousal and child abuse. Yet, when a woman is in the grips of a violent situation without the resources to extract herself, it is important to consider the possibility of diminished responsibility.

In many cases, however, the Victim must take as much responsibility for the situation as the Rescuer or Persecutor. Especially important in the Rescuer/Victim situation is that Rescuing people eventually causes anger. The Rescuer gets fed up with doing things that he or she does not really want to do, and the Victim gets fed up with being treated as someone who cannot take care of himself.

Inevitably, the Rescuer will persecute the Victim, or the Victim will persecute the Rescuer. Anger will overflow in all directions.

When we play any of these three roles, the emotionally literate thing to do is to rectify the situation, make things better. Let's start with Rescues.

STEP 9

Apologizing for Our Mistakes

Remedying a Rescue.

Tempting though it is to want to do things for others, hard though it may be to say no, learning not to rescue is hugely important for anyone who wants to preserve and nurture meaningful relationships. When we find ourselves playing the role of Rescuer in a repetitive cycle, it is important to rectify our mistake by recognizing it, stopping, and apologizing. Here is how it is done:

"When I (describe action), I rescued you (1) because I did not really want to do it, or (2) because I believed that I was doing more than my share. I apologize and will do better next time. Do you accept my apology?"

This needs to be handled with care. Finding out that someone has been rescuing you can be quite humiliating. Also, learning that someone close to you no longer wants to do something he or she has been doing for some time can feel like abandonment. It is important to approach this gently and very important to take proper responsibility for the mistake while being as nurturing as possible.

To stop rescuing, you have to clarify what you want or do not want to do, and what is fair. And of course, you have to decide exactly what it is you are doing that constitutes a Rescue.

The best way to do that is to ask yourself questions about what you are doing and whether you should or should not keep doing it. For example you may need to ask yourself:

- Do I want to continue this conversation?

- Do I want to have sex?

- Do I want to fix the car?

- Do I want to go to the ball game?

- Do I want to spend time with my husband's family?

- Do I want to cook tonight?

Sometimes your Rescue may involve doing more than your share. If that is the case, you have to ask yourself what constitutes a fair share of the effort involved in a relationship. The questions you ask yourself will be similar to these:

- Is it fair for me to do the dishes if Mary cooks, or should I also sweep the floor?

- Is it fair that I always initiate sex?

- Should I always pay for dinner when we go out?

- Is it fair that I always pick up the kids from school?

- Sharon has been talking to me about her problems with her sister for months now. Should I let her go on or tell her I am bored with this subject?

In other words, you have to learn to know what you want to do or what you think amounts to a fair distribution of a relationship's responsibilities. Let me clarify what I mean using Peter and Jacquie's example:

- When Jacquie cooks dinner every night while Peter watches TV, she is doing more than her share—and therefore rescuing—even if she likes to cook and is willing.

- When she cleans up the dishes because Peter says to leave them until next morning, she is doing something she hates, so she is rescuing.

ERRORS MADE WHILE APOLOGIZING

Giving lip service. The importance of apology has gained universal recognition.

Alcoholics Anonymous lists making amends as one of the twelve steps of its program. People who are in frequent contact with the public, such as flight attendants and bank clerks, are taught to apologize as a way to quiet angry customers, when necessary.

Apologies can be facile and meaningless. It isn't enough to just say "Gee, I'm sorry," or even "Honestly, I am sorry," if there isn't real regret behind the apology.

Peter, for instance, apologized often and profusely to Jacquie. However, he barely realized what he was saying and certainly was only minimally sincere. He knew it pacified Jacquie, so he went ahead and apologized whenever he got in trouble with her. She would accept his apology but within days—maybe hours—she felt as if she had been had.

An apology has to be heartfelt and has to be for specific behavior, or it is meaningless and ultimately ineffective. Words alone do not change things or soothe the aggrieved party. *And, of course, an apology that is not followed by a change of behavior will quickly prove meaningless.*

Blaming the Victim. When we discover that we have been rescuing someone, it is easy to get mad at him. Jacquie is an example of someone, who, after much rescuing, was furious at Peter. Attacking another person because we are angry is rarely the right response and is certainly the wrong one when you decide to stop being a Rescuer.

Keep in mind that it takes two to tango, but only one to change the dynamics of a relationship. Getting angry can hurt your relationship with the person you have been rescuing, which is why it is important to stop rescuing *before* your anger builds up. Do this with a gentle and nurturing explanation rather than an abrupt withdrawal. Above all, do not blame the Victim for your mistake. Don't forget, rescuing is a mistake on your part and not necessarily on the part of the Rescued/Victim.

CASE STUDY

Both Sides of Apology

Here is an example of a properly delivered and accepted apology:

Laura frequently found herself having unwanted sex with her husband Brian. He would tell her that he had a tough day at work and needed her, or that he was all wound up and could not get to sleep if she did not have sex with him. If she refused him, he would become angry or pout. At that point, no matter how Laura felt, she would give in.

Laura came to me and asked how she could change her relationship with Brian. She loved him, she said, but she felt as though he was taking advantage of her. Lately she had started resenting him and had even thought about leaving him. She thought that some emotional literacy training might be helpful and she came to me for the tools.

After talking to her for a while, I could see that Laura was a habitual Rescuer, not just with Brian but in all sorts of situations. With Brian, her worse Rescue was that even when she did not want to have sex with him, she did it anyway. Now she was feeling used and wanted to persecute him by leaving him.

I explained to her the importance of taking responsibility for her actions and explained how to frame an apology for being a Rescuer.

I told her that she needed to stop rescuing in all sorts of places but that it would be a good idea to start with Brian.

Here is what happened next:

Friday evening Laura told Brian that she would like to have a special Saturday night dinner to talk about something important. Brian seemed wary and somewhat alarmed.

"I want to talk about something I've been thinking about," said Laura. "I'll make an early dinner and we can have a relaxed conversation."

Saturday evening came, and Laura, after they had finished eating, took a deep breath and began.

"Brian, I have been feeling bad about something between us, may I tell you about it?"

Brian shrugged. Although he smiled, he was scared. "Well, that seems to be why we're here," he said warily.

"Okay, I am worried that you are going to be upset about what I am going to say. Here it goes," she gulped. "I feel bad that I've been making love with you lately and some of the times I didn't really feel like it."

She eyed Brian nervously, trying to gauge his response. Seeing nothing in his face she continued, "Maybe I didn't make it clear enough that I didn't want to. I guess I gave you mixed messages, and I'm sorry."

Brian erupted. "What are you trying to say? You don't want to sleep with me?"

"No, I'm not saying I never want to have sex, I just mean that I feel that we have sex when you are in the mood, not when I am, and I don't want to go on making love when I'm not in the mood. I'm not blaming you for what I've done up until now, going along with your wishes and ignoring mine. I am trying to take responsibility for that, but I also want to change things."

"Well, it sounds like you're not attracted to me, as if I'm your sexual charity case . . ."

"No, no. I am attracted to you. But sometimes I'm tired or preoccupied or just not feeling sexual. I just don't feel like having sex."

"Well, are you *ever* in the mood? It seems to me that if I didn't start things, you never would."

"It's true I don't usually think to initiate sex, but sometimes when you do I really like it. Other times I'm tired and not really into it. I don't want to continue having sex like that, when I don't really feel like it. It makes me ashamed of myself and sometimes even angry at you. Maybe if we didn't have sex when I'm not in the mood as often, I might be in the mood more often."

Brian listened quietly as Laura continued.

"The point is that it's not your fault. I take responsibility for my decisions to go along. But I want to do things differently from now on. I just want things to be good between us, as good as they can be, because I love you."

Brian looked at her warily, "Well, I'm just going to leave you alone. I don't want to be your sexual charity project. If you want to make love, you can let me know."

With that, he walked over the couch and turned on the baseball game. Laura was very upset, though I had warned her that Brian might be quite defensive at first. Once the initial shock subsided, however, he would probably relax and accept her feelings and proposal.

She went to the bedroom where she knew she wouldn't be heard and called her sister up to unburden herself about the upsetting situation. Then she read a novel in bed. She decided to let the dishes wait until morning. When Brian came to bed, she pretended to be asleep to avoid a confrontation. He got into bed without touching her at all and, after lying awake awhile, fell asleep. Once she heard his regular breathing pattern, Laura moved over and held him close until she fell asleep. She was worried but kept reminding herself that things would get better.

CHANGE OF HEART

In the morning, Brian, who had noticed that Laura cuddled with him throughout the night, was aloof, reading the paper and drinking coffee. Then he unexpectedly left, announcing last-minute Sunday plans with some male friends.

When Brian came home that evening, he handed Laura a small, scraggly bunch of wildflowers he had picked at the last minute on the way home. She kissed him appreciatively. For a moment Brian wanted to grab Laura and kiss her. At that point he stopped himself, feeling vaguely humiliated. She sensed his turmoil and went into the kitchen to fix some tea.

Brian sat on the couch, wrestling with his feelings of humiliation. After all, he thought, she's not blaming me. He remembered a few times early in the relationship when she had wanted to have sex and he was too tired. He decided to try not to take the situation personally.

"Let's eat out tonight," he announced impulsively.

At dinner Brian said, "Can I tell you how I feel?" Laura agreed eagerly.

"When you told me about the unwanted sex last night I felt angry at first, and then scared that you weren't attracted to me anymore. Then I became sad that we have been having sex without you enjoying it."

Laura nodded.

Brian continued. "I accept your apology for going along. Let's see if we can have sex only when we both want it."

That night, after dinner, they kissed in bed. Brian decided not to try to have intercourse, and Laura fell asleep in his arms. He felt frustrated and lay awake for a while, but it was reassuring to feel Laura nuzzle against him in her sleep.

It took a few months before the tensions between Laura and Brian subsided. Gradually, however, he accepted her wishes and got over his feelings of embarrassment and abandonment. She, for her part, made an effort to take sexual initiative once in a while, especially on weekends when she had more energy.

Through conversations and compromise, they got out of the destructive Rescue pattern that was secretly threatening their sex life and, ultimately, their marriage.

REMEDYING A PERSECUTION

The role of Persecutor is much more obvious than Rescuer. There is no need to explain why apologies for persecuting are important!

Some people are habitual Persecutors, stuck in an angry, blaming role. Nothing works, everything is somebody else's fault, and they are constantly angry at something or someone.

The Persecutor is the mirror image of the Victim for whom nothing works, and everything is somebody else's fault.

When we play the Persecutor we are irritable and testy. We may insult, mock, discount, ignore, interrupt, yell, lecture, or constantly contradict others. Or, we may lie.

These are all power plays, and Persecution is essentially a matter of using power plays to control others. In subtler ways, rescuing or playing the Victim are power plays as well because their purpose is also to manipulate others.

Rather than being deeply stuck in the role of Persecutor, most people will switch from normal, reasonable behavior into the Persecutor role for a transaction or two. Then, unaware of the effects of their actions, return to normal as if nothing had happened.

Each one of the Persecutory injuries, small or large, accumulates and creates resentments. Eventually they proliferate into further injurious actions and even stronger feelings. Most people will absorb these incidents and believe that they have dealt with them, which is what emotional numbing is all about.

But if we are to live well-managed emotional lives, we need to set all of these injuries straight. That is done by acknowledging our mistakes and apologizing for them.

Persecution can be very obvious or very subtle or somewhere in between. The remedying of Persecution follows the same pattern as the Remedying of Rescues. Let me give an example:

CASE STUDY

Messy and Neat

Beth has just moved in with Richard. Beth is neat and orderly. She is also very concerned about her possessions. For her, all her record albums, every book, her clothes, even her magazines, are little treasures that she has carefully picked out and preserved, through her many moves from apartment to apartment.

Richard is an unrepentant creator of chaos. He lives in a pile of papers and boxes of new gizmos with clothing strewn all about.

Richard unwittingly tends to put his stuff on top of Beth's stuff. This makes Beth furious. She is very detail-oriented and always notices where she places her things. She would never throw her coat on top of Richard's shoes or crumple his new magazines. She is also under a lot of stress because of conflicts with her boss and concern over her depressed brother. She finds herself becoming more and more angry at Richard's carelessness.

Because she is not sure how to approach the problem, she often puts on a mockingly furious tone when she complains to Richard "Oh darling . . . look whose greasy car manual I found on top of my favorite pumps. . . . Naughty, naughty."

Richard glances in her direction, vaguely aware that he's being reprimanded. But the problem continues. Eventually, Beth becomes very angry. "Damn it, Richard, why do you do this? Look at my shoes, they're crushed! I searched for almost an hour for this sweater of mine that you threw in with your laundry! Leave my things alone!"

"They're all over my room," Richard retaliates.

"Your room? If I can't put my things down on one chair in *our* living room, then I'm sorry I moved in with you. Maybe I should move out so you can have *your* room back."

In the back of her mind, Beth is growing uneasy about the harpielike posture she has drifted into. What went wrong?

From a position of Emotional Literacy, here is what went wrong:

She should have dealt with her feelings from the beginning in a calm tone, using an action/feeling statement, after getting Richard's attention. Instead, she started to complain timidly with a faintly critical joke, which only confused Richard and didn't get her message across. Essentially, she rescued him, going along with his messiness. Her complaints became hostile when she got fed up with being ignored.

Here is the approach she must use:

Realizing her mistake, Beth asks Richard when he will be free to talk. He suggests after lunch, and when the time comes, the dialogue proceeds like this:

"Richard, I want to apologize about something."

"What?"

"You know how we've been fighting when you do something to my things that I don't like."

Richard raises his eyebrows and makes a *tsk* sound, indicating that he is well aware of the "fights," which to him feel more like blitzkriegs over trivia.

"Well, I feel that I've been persecuting you unfairly. I never really sat down and calmly asked you to do things differently, and I guess I can't expect you to change your ways overnight.

"I've been really frustrated and upset about my boss and my brother, and I'm probably visiting some of my frustration on you. I'm sorry for being so hostile and impatient."

With this approach his response might well be, "Okay I didn't realize how serious you are about your stuff. I'll try to do better. I apologize for calling our living room 'my room.' I guess I should have listened to you more closely about your things also."

GETTING OUT OF THE VICTIM ROLE

Last but certainly not least in this catalogue of corrective procedures is the Remedying of Victim behavior.

One way to regain some power when we feel completely defeated and powerless is to play games in the role of the Victim.

One of the first games that Eric Berne discovered and which illustrates that principle beautifully is "Why don't you? Yes, but."

In this game a person in the Victim role hooks one or more people into giving advice on a problem that he considers hopeless. For example, Bruce hates his job and his boss and is sure that his coworkers hate him. What is he to do? He asks a number of his friends. They try to help:

T: "Why don't you quit and find another job?"

B: "Yes that's a good idea, but there are no jobs that pay as well as this one."

N: "Why don't you get a union mediator and work it out with your boss?"

B: "Yes, I thought of that but the union mediator right now is a woman, and she doesn't understand these kinds of problems."

F: "Why don't you go to a meditation weekend and develop a white light around you that protects you from harm?"

B: "Yeah sure, have you seen how much those weekends cost?"

T: "I guess you're right; it's a pretty hopeless situation. If I was in your place I'd want to kill myself."

B: "I know there's no use. I guess you guys can't help me. It's really up to me, isn't it? Let's have a stiff one."

At this point everybody is depressed. Bruce is gloating over his power to bring down a roomful of drinking buddies, and his gloomy view of the world is vindicated.

The next day, Bruce bought the book *Achieving Emotional Literacy* and read about the Victim role. He realized that he had a tendency to be depressed and feel hopeless and that the best way to get out of this role is to apologize.

The next time he got together with his buddies, he startled everybody by saying: "Listen guys, I want to apologize about something."

Everyone is stunned into silence.

B: "You know I feel that when I start complaining about my job and asking for advice and not taking it, that I am really acting like a powerless victim and I realize it must be a bummer. I apologize. I'm not going to do that anymore."

T: "What is this, twelve-step amends or something?"

B: "Something like that. I am serious though, and I want you guys to accept my apology. Deal?"

STEP 10

Accepting or Rejecting Apologies

There is obviously a great deal of skill involved in making a heartfelt apology. Few people realize, however, that there is an equally important skill involved in accepting, or rejecting, an apology once it is given.

Ed, who has been talking too much in a staff meeting, is told by one of his coworkers, Sue, to shut up when a much less sharp response would have been more appropriate. Later, Sue comes into Ed's office and apologizes. Ed, however, is still unhappy at being belittled in the meeting. The apology somehow isn't working.

How does he handle the coworker's apology without accepting it just yet?

The most common mistake in accepting an apology is forgiving too easily. In response to the apology of his fellow worker, Ed might say, "No problem, that's okay."

However, by doing this he is probably trying to avoid the humiliation of feeling patronized. Or he may even be trying to rescue his coworker from her responsibilities. It is best not to do that.

An apology doesn't heal much if it is accepted without reflection. If someone gives you a perfunctory apology, and you say, "No problem," you will probably feel just as bad as before. You have simply accepted the apology because you have learned what's socially expected of you. Even if the apology is heartfelt and sincere, you can render it useless by accepting it in a perfunctory way.

The emotionally appropriate response is always to think about the apology and decide whether you want to accept it or not.

There are two very valid reasons why an apology might not work:

- It seems insincere.

- It doesn't specify the injury incurred.

148

If it seems insincere, Ed can say: "Listen Sue, I appreciate your coming in and apologizing to me, but it doesn't seem that you really mean it. Are you really sorry about what you said? I had been talking too much in the meeting, fair enough. But it hurts to be treated like that. I would like to believe you really regret the way you talked to me."

The approach Ed took here is to acknowledge but not accept the coworker's apology.

But let's say that Sue came into Ed's office and said earnestly, "Listen, Ed, I'm sorry about this afternoon."

Ed could accept this but he might feel uneasy. What is she apologizing for?

He could ask, "What do you mean? What are you apologizing for?"

Sue might answer, "Oh, about being angry at you and not offering you any coffee at the break."

Clearly this isn't going to work.

Ed should say something like, "Sue, I noticed about the coffee, but what really hurt me is the way you told me to shut up. If you want to apologize that is where the apology is needed."

Sue is surprised. "Oh . . . well, you're right, that was uncalled for. I guess I thought you had pretty thick skin. . . . I'm sorry. I shouldn't have spoken to you like that."

Now Ed can relax, this is an apology he can accept. All this is to say that a person might need a more extensive apology than the one that is offered.

REJECTED APOLOGIES

Some further examples of rejected apologies:

• A woman's heart was broken when her fiancé called off their engagement. She was devastated and humiliated. Days later he came to apologize, but she was much too furious and hurt to accept. It was only months later, after several long discussions about his decision to break off their engagement, that she was finally able to accept.

• A victim of a long string of large impulsive purchases, Peter is unable to forgive his wife. He needs a much more extensive apology for the years of financial worries she has caused him and some concrete assurances of her intention to change her ways. There may be nothing she can do to remedy her mistakes.

• Claude's friend André apologizes for accepting an invitation to a dinner party on his behalf, without asking him. Claude is beginning to feel that André is ignoring his distaste for social outings with new people. He always thinks each party is an exception. He refuses the apology because André does not seem to care that he always puts Claude in awkward situations.

These examples illustrate that it is an error to accept an apology if it doesn't truly make you feel better. You should explain to the person apologizing why it falls short. Then the person can try to apologize in a way that acknowledges the true nature of the mistake.

BASHING THE RIGHTEOUS

Another error is what I call "Bashing the Righteous."

Let's go back to Ed and Sue.

Let's say that Sue earnestly apologizes to Ed for her nasty tone of voice when she told him to shut up.

Ed now sees an opportunity to get even, to hurt her the way that he has been hurt.

"Well, it's about time you apologized," he might say. "I resent it and I am very angry with you. You are such a bitch sometimes!"

If you are trying to build Emotional Literacy, this won't do either. If Ed is angry he can use an action/feeling statement to deal with his reaction: "It makes me angry that you spoke to me the way you did. I also feel embarrassed. But I appreciate your apology. Please don't do it again."

Sometimes an apology does not work. Usually this is because the injury was too large to be dispelled by a simple apology. Perhaps the victim needs an explanation or some form of retribution.

For example, the man who has been financially damaged by his wife needs for her to explain how she has changed and that she will get a job to bring them back into solvency.

Claude needs André to admit that he has accepted invitations for Claude hoping to break him of his shyness. He promises to stop doing that and to check with Claude about every social event that involves both of them.

It is important to keep in mind that the ultimate purpose of an apology is to give the Victim a chance to feel better about the way he or she has been hurt.

STEP 11

Asking for Forgiveness

An emotionally literate way of apologizing for an action that has deeply hurt another person.

Garden variety emotional errors occur frequently. Because of that, it is a part of emotional housekeeping to keep track of them and clean them up when needed.

Sometimes, however, we make hurtful mistakes that can cause long-term damage. In that case it is important to make a major apology and even, if necessary, beg for forgiveness.

"I apologize for (action); it was wrong and I regret having hurt you. Will you forgive me?"

CASE STUDY

Begging Forgiveness

A dramatic example of begging for forgiveness is the story of Rose and Edgar, two sixty-years-olds who were about to celebrate their fortieth wedding anniversary when they attended one of my emotional literacy workshops.

After we discussed the power of apologies, Edgar raised his hand. He declared that he needed to do some emotional work with Rose.

He explained why: Thirty-five years ago, on the evening of the birth of their son, he'd sex with another woman.

It happened right after he saw the baby and visited Rose in the recovery room. He left the hospital late at night, but was too excited to go directly home.

Instead, he went into a neighborhood bar to have a drink. As he sat enjoying a double whisky, he noticed a young woman coworker. He told her about his new son and offered to buy her a drink. One drink led to another and before he knew it, they were in her apartment having sex.

When he left the next morning, Edgar was overcome with guilt. He felt terrible that he had cheated on his wife and impulsively told Rose what he had done.

Rose was devastated by the news. Even though he assured his wife that he had been stupidly drunk and never wanted to see the woman again, Rose was inconsolable and unforgiving.

For the next thirty-five years, virtually every argument between them contained references to the incident. Every time Rose felt Edgar was taking her for granted, or did not give her the attention she should have, she would bring up the dreaded incident.

They were both very distressed about this. After all these years the incident was still like a thorn in both of their sides, one that they had pretty much given up trying to remove.

On this occasion, Edgar thought that he needed to do something he had never done: Take full responsibility for his infidelity and beg Rose for forgiveness.

He did this in the most touching way. In front of the entire class, Edgar got on his knees and grasped Rose's hand. With tears in his eyes he began to speak.

"Rose," he asked, "May I speak to you about something?"

"Yes," she agreed.

"Rose, I know that I have apologized a hundred times about this and I have complained that it doesn't seem to work."

She nodded.

"I realize from this discussion that even though I apologized, my apologies have been hollow, and I am not surprised that they haven't worked."

Again, she nodded.

"I understand why. It is because I have not really acknowledged how much I hurt you. I really didn't want to accept that I had hurt you so much. So I made excuses and never stopped to experience your pain."

He wiped his eyes and asked, "May I apologize now?"

At this point there wasn't a dry eye in the room, including Rose's. She nodded again, this time warmly, covering his hands with hers.

"Rose, after all these years, I realize how much what I did hurt you. I am so sorry that I did it and so sorry that it took me so long to realize the extent of your pain. Would you please forgive me?" Rose agreed and they hugged, surrounded by fellow emotional literacy students.

One year later I happened to meet Edgar. I asked him how things were. He told me that they had just had a wonderful anniversary celebration, with many friends and family.

"By the way," he added, "Rose has never brought up that incident again."

STEP 12

Granting or Denying Forgiveness

After hearing the apology, this step shows how to grant forgiveness, deny it, or postpone it.

After hearing an apology and thoughtful soul-searching, we can either:

- Grant forgiveness,

- Postpone pending additional amends, or

- Deny it.

People assume that if they offer a heartfelt apology for a particularly wretched misdeed, the injured party will or ought to forgive. However, to be forgiven is an enormous gift, and it cannot always be granted. Forgiveness depends entirely on whether our hearts respond in a forgiving manner to the apology, and it is not possible or advisable to force the heart in matters of love, hate, or forgiveness.

Consequently, it is as important in emotionally literate relationships that we properly grant or decline forgiveness as that we ask for it. Sadly it may at times happen that forgiveness will not be granted under any circumstances.

Karla spent five years recovering from the devastating heartbreak of an extremely acrimonious divorce in which Bill abruptly left her for his secret lover of six months and then proceeded without success (because Karla had a very good lawyer) to prevent her from receiving a proper division of their assets. Her pain lasted a full five years, but eventually she overcame her distress, met another man, and remarried happily. Still, even today Karla's eyes tear when she talks about the events of the past. Very soon after the divorce, Bill's relationship fell apart and he attempted to reconnect with Karla to be friends. Karla was completely unwilling even to speak to Bill, but over the years, through common friends who liked them both and for the sake of their teenage son, she began to speak to him on the phone occasionally. She had long ago concluded that their marriage had been very flawed and that terminating it had been good. But she could not forget or forgive the lies that Bill had told and the financial maneuvers she had had to fight. Through friends, she let it be known that no relationship was possible without an apology.

Bill, eager to reestablish the friendship, wrote her a note:

Dear Karla,
  I want to apologize for my part in hurting your feelings.
I am sorry.

Bill

When Karla received that note, she was furious. Was she supposed to take this hastily written note as an apology? She didn't even bother to respond.

Eventually Bill called her. After some polite preliminaries, he asked: "Did you get my note?"

"Yes."

"Well?"

"Well, what?"

"Do you forgive me?"

"For what?"

"What do you mean, for what? I thought you wanted an apology!"

"Oh, I see. . . . well, I guess I don't forgive you."

"Why not?"

"You haven't really apologized."

"What about my note?"

"Your note was okay as a start. What are you apologizing for?"

"For hurting you."

"I need an apology for what you did."

"What do you mean?"

"You lied, you were cruel, you tried to cheat me."

"I don't know about that. That's a matter of opinion. . . ."

"Well, what are you apologizing for then? It's not enough to say that you had a part in hurting me. What part did you have? Unless you can acknowledge what you did to hurt me, I am not really interested in an apology."

There the conversation ended. Several years later Bill again wanted to make things right. He wrote another note:

Dear Karla,

I thought about what we talked about and I agree that I lied to you, but it was because I thought you would be more upset if you knew the truth, and financially I was afraid that you would rip me off. I am sorry if I hurt your feelings and I apologize.

Again Karla was less than satisfied. Bill's justifications for what he now acknowledged doing detracted from the apology enough that her heart did not open, and she could see no reason to let Bill back into her life. There seemed to be no acknowledgment of how badly he had hurt her.

She wrote him back the following note:

Bill,

I got your letter and I see that you are making an effort to make things right. However, you are spending more words in giving excuses for what you did than in acknowledging what a brutal and painful experience I went through. We both made mistakes that we are paying for. I was not perfect. But if you want us to be friends, I will have to be convinced that you realize how you hurt me, how much of the pain I suffered was caused by your actions. And then you have to feel and communicate some sorrow and even guilt to me. I need to experience that kind of feeling from you, and until then I feel and believe it's best for me that we keep our distance.

Karla

There the matter was left. Bill may eventually recognize what he needs to do or he may decide he can't or won't, but Karla is taking care of herself emotionally by refusing to grant forgiveness prematurely. If she softened and let Bill off the hook without feeling the healing satisfaction that comes from a heart-felt apology, she will never really open to Bill and their "friend-ship" will be a painful sham. The process of apology and forgiveness is extremely important in an emotionally literate life and is worth pursuing to sometimes excruciating extremes.

As people become skilled in the use of these techniques, they lose their initial awkwardness. They become part of every-day emotional housekeeping, like raking leaves, walking the dog, or flossing teeth.

Once assimilated, they contribute to a well-ordered emotional life in which emotions are acknowledged and given their proper place as a source of power and well-being.

But the rewards of Emotional Literacy are more than just a tidy emotional house. When our emotions are clear and fully expressed and other people's feelings matter as much to us as our own, life becomes powerfully moving and at times truly joyous. It is then that the rewards of an emotionally literate life show their promise.

SUMMARY

Taking Responsibility

You'll find that the hardest part of becoming emotionally literate is owning up to the mistakes you've made in your relationships, but this is an indispensable step.

First, you must admit to yourself that you have made a mistake. Then you have to admit your mistake to others. Next, you must feel true regret and convey that to the person you have hurt. Finally, you must make amends.

We make emotional mistakes when we let ourselves be drawn into one of three roles: Rescuer, Persecutor, or Victim.

As a Rescuer, you do things for people that you don't want to do and that they should do for themselves.

As a Persecutor, you become angry and self-righteously attack other people, often people you have tried to rescue.

As a Victim, you either allow yourself to be taken care of by a Rescuer or attacked by a Persecutor, all the while whining that you can do nothing about the situation.

If you have acted as a Rescuer, Persecutor, or Victim, you must apologize to the people you have hurt and resolve to act like a responsible adult in the future. If you have been hurt, you must learn the proper way to grant, postpone or deny forgiveness.

7

LOVING, PARENTING, AND WORKING

Emotional Literacy has value in nearly every aspect of daily life. If you practice the steps that you have just read, chances are that your relationships with almost everyone will improve. Most important is that you'll see changes in your relationship with yourself as a result of altering your methods of dealing with others. You will find that these techniques not only clarify the world around us, they clarify the world inside of us as well.

Although the advice you have just read is a comprehensive program for improving your Emotional Literacy in every area of your life, there are three situations that require special attention: loving relationships, raising children, and workplace relations.

Let's begin with loving relationships.

EMOTIONAL LITERACY
IN LOVING RELATIONSHIPS

Finding and maintaining a good partnership is difficult. Many people are discovering that even though the old system of domination/submission is largely obsolete, they still fall back into it unless they learn and work hard to maintain a new approach.

In today's relationships people give lip service to the idea that there needs to be a partnership between equals. In actual practice, however, people are genuinely confused about how to make it work. In relationships between men and women, men still tend to dominate, while women find it hard to assert themselves. As the new saying goes, "Men are from Mars, women are from Venus."

It is no wonder that more and more people are simply giving up and living alone.

That is no solution, of course, unless living alone is specifically what you want. The answer is to pursue a relationship and Emotional Literacy at the same time. You can do that no matter how long you have been together but you must adopt the guidelines for an emotionally literate relationship, which are

- a conviction that both partners are equals,

- a commitment to honesty,

- an agreement not to power play each other.

Equality, honesty, and agreements. My recommendation for those who want an emotionally literate relationship is to quickly establish a cooperative contract based on equality and honesty. A cooperative relationship will ensue when neither person tries to manipulate the other with power plays and neither does anything he or she doesn't want to do. Instead, both partners gently and lovingly ask for everything they want until satisfied, while both partners listen empathically to hear what each other needs.

Of course, mistakes will be made and apologies and amends will be necessary. These ground rules will require that you overcome the old established patterns of power playing, rescuing, and lying. These changes are not easy and will not come overnight, but you will find that the energy and optimism released in this process will invigorate any relationship, new or old.

Equality. Equality is based on the idea that both people need to have equal rights and should make an equal contribution toward the relationship's success. The idea that people have equal rights doesn't mean that people can't differ from each other for a relationship to work. Especially between men and women, who are in many ways different, it simply means that those differences don't give one person privilege over the other.

Equality does not mean that both partners have to work and earn the same or that expenses and housework are shared fifty-fifty. Equality in an emotionally literate relationship means that both partners contribute what they have to offer in such a way that both feel satisfied. If they become dissatisfied with the other's contribution they must feel free to say so with the assurance that their partners will work toward a fair compromise.

Honesty. Honesty is the most important agreement in a relationship between equals.

No one enters into a serious relationship expecting to be lied to. In fact, it is assumed that two people in love should not lie to each other at all.

Many relationships are consecrated in ceremonies in which vows are made: "For richer or for poorer, in sickness or health, to honor, love, and cherish . . ." These vows don't normally include a vow to be completely honest. Small wonder since by that time, in most relationships, at least one of the participants has already lied about something. Sometimes both have. Even in the most honest of relationships, something has probably gone awry and been swept under the rug. Maybe she has always longed for more strokes about her looks, but felt too embarrassed to ask for them. Or perhaps he has not been honest about his dissatisfaction with their lovemaking.

Even the smallest lie or secret has a damaging effect because it can be the seed for further and bigger dishonesty.

If you are well into a long-term relationship, the situation becomes more delicate. In trying to clean the slate of lies, there may be dark secrets that could truly upset the other person. Maybe there has been a one-night stand or even a full-blown affair with a third person. Or maybe one partner has recklessly spent money from the joint account without telling the other. Maybe there is some long-term unhappiness or deep dissatisfaction with the other's looks, intelligence, sense of humor, or sexual style. If that is the case it may be a good idea to get rid of these secrets with the help of a third person; a trusted friend, a therapist, or a minister.

Such lies of omission, usually about sex, money, or appearance cannot be allowed to remain secret in an emotionally literate relationship. They must be revealed. If a partner with a secret does not reveal it and the other partner finds out, it is my experience that the lie hurts the partner more than the misdeed itself. How long the secret has been kept, how many others know about it, and all the ramifications of the lie are often so devastating that they can permanently damage or wreck the relationship. It is difficult to forgive missteps, but far more difficult to forgive the lies that surround them.

Even people who claim that they would "rather not know" if their partner has strayed, will likely find the truth extremely humiliating and hurtful. When we condone secrets and say "I'd rather not know," we have probably not anticipated how terrible it would feel to unwittingly discover such a secret. That is why lying is so damaging and why it needs to be removed from any emotionally literate relationship.

With that in mind, let me offer some agreements to create an Emotional Literate relationship:

• **Equality takes two:** Keep in mind that an emotionally literate relationship requires both partners to work at it as equals. To do this you must grant each other equal rights and expect equal responsibilities.

• **Cooperation is the key:** Agree with your partner to have a relationship of equality free of power plays, especially lies and Rescues. Make it clear that you want a relationship in which both of you ask for everything you want and don't do anything that you don't want to do.

Start talking about a cooperative relationship right away. If you are getting involved in a new relationship, begin talking about this notion as soon as you feel that the relationship has long-term potential.

This is especially important if you are in love, where everything is seen through a rose-colored mist. Just talking frankly about issues will bring clarity and reality to your budding relationship.

Fran and John are in love. They are lying in the grass, warmed by the spring sunshine on their day off. Both have agreed that they would like to get married. She has been married before with bad results and wants to do better this time.

F: "John, can I bring up something that I would like us to talk about before we get married?"

J: "Sure, what is it.?"

F: "I have been reading a book about how to have an emotionally literate relationship."

J: "*What* kind of a relationship?"

F: "It's a relationship in which you are emotionally involved and aware. A cooperative relationship where both people agree ahead of time about some things."

J: "What things?"

F: "Well, this book talks about an honest relationship between equals and I really liked what it says; the idea is that we agree to always say what we want and to make sure that we never get pressured into doing things we don't want to do."

J: "I like that. But it seems like we already to it. Don't you think?"

F: "I know we both want to, but sometimes I think we don't, actually."

163

J: "Like when?"

F: "I think we both lie about what we want and go along with the other person sometimes. Like this morning when we went to the Blue Barn for breakfast. I really wanted to go to the Brick Shack, but I lied because I wanted to please you."

J: "Lied? Isn't that what being generous is all about?

F: "In *Achieving Emotional Literacy* it's called Rescuing, and it's not good because after a while the person who Rescues gets angry. Usually it's me who goes along with you."

J: "I know you do and I love that about you; you spoil me. Does that mean you are going to get mad at me later?"

F: "Could be, and I really don't want that. And maybe there is stuff you are going along with that I don't know about. Is there?"

J: "Well a couple of things, but I don't mind . . ."

F: "Well I think Steiner is right; it would be better if we were completely honest about that kind of a thing. What are these things you go along with?"

J: "Why do you want me to look for things to complain about? I love you!"

F: "I just want us to learn to have a cooperative, honest relationship."

J: "I'll try." He thinks for a moment. "Okay. the truth is I would rather not meet all your girlfriends and hang out with them the way we do . . ."

F: "Really."

J: "It's just not something I'm into. It's not very interesting. I mean, I want to meet them, but I don't want to make a special point to spend time with each of them. I don't have the time to get to know every one of your friends, you know. Also . . . I'm sorry, is this too hard on you?"

F: "A little, but it's okay, let's go ahead. Thanks for asking."

J: "Okay, if you're sure." With a concerned look he continues. "I'm really glad you introduced me to your parents. But I'm not that much into family things, like your aunt's Thanksgiving party. That was a bit much for me, meeting all these people who don't seem that important to us."

F: "Okay" she answers in a subdued voice. "I mean, I'm disappointed and embarrassed now to think that I introduced you to everyone so enthusiastically and you were wishing you were somewhere else."

J: "It wasn't that bad, I'd just rather pass."

F: "Well. I really do like spending time with my family. I have ever since I was a kid. But if you don't want to come along I'll just go by myself."

A thoughtful silence ensues. John begins again. "I'll tell you what, why don't you tell me which events are really important to you and I'll go with you to those. Maybe you can go early and I'll meet you a little later, so I don't have to stay as long."

F: "That sounds fair."

He holds her tightly around her waist. They both have a bit to think about, but Fran was proud of herself for initiating an emotionally literate dialogue, and John was relieved to have gotten out of some unwanted social obligations.

You may wonder why two happy young lovers should start discussing the small dissatisfactions which at the moment seem wholly unimportant compared to the wonderful love they feel for each other. But these are the things which, when the rosy light of new love begins to soften and reality returns, often drive apart couples who once thought nothing could ever come between them.

Fran learned this the hard way with her first marriage. She is right to take the initiative and start a dialogue about ground rules which establish a level of honesty and awareness that later will be very important to avoid another emotional disaster.

- **Honesty is the best policy:** Does your partner know enough about you to have an honest picture of who you are? If not, be brave and fill in the picture. Honesty is frightening, but it pays off when it builds a stronger, more intimate relationship.

If you have information that you are keeping secret from your partner plan to tell your partner as soon as possible. Hoping for a better time to bring it up usually doesn't work because that better time rarely comes. Instead of waiting, just do it now.

Realize that honesty involves saying what you want, talking about how you feel, and asking for apologies when you can't let go of a partner's misdeed.

Sloan and Carol have been married for a couple of years. Theirs is a good relationship that dates back to high school, where they were voted cutest couple by their senior class. In a romantic moment Carol tells Sloan how good it feels to her that they haven't had sex with anyone but each other.

Sloan swallows hard. It turns out that three years ago, during a six month separation in which they reassessed their relationship, he had a one-night stand with an acquaintance of Carol's. He did not tell Carol, telling himself that it was not part of their agreement to do so. Now, however, he feels that he must speak up:

"Carol, how do you feel about the idea that if we are going to have a long-term relationship there should be no secrets or lies between us?"

Carol looks alarmed. "Why, have you been lying to me about something?!"

Sloan looks into Carol's eyes. "No, Carol, I don't think so, and I don't want to start now. Let's sit down. There is something that I never realized until now that I need to tell you. Can I tell you now?"

"What is it, for God's sake!"

Sloan walks Carol over to the couch. Looking in her eyes

he asks, "Do you remember the time we were separated back in college?"

"Yes," she answers, beginning to realize what he's about to say.

"Well, I never stopped thinking about you during those months, but I also thought you might decide that you didn't want to be with me anymore. I was trying to get used to whatever might happen, and I was very depressed. One night, I went on a date with Suzie Green."

"My old friend Susan?" she said with a shrill sound entering her voice. She always felt a little insecure beside the beautiful and popular Susan.

"Yeah. I think I should tell you about that date."

"Oh God, Sloan!"

"I'm sorry. I didn't think I would have to tell you. But after what you said about never having other lovers I realize now that I have to. Anyway, I want you to know everything about me." As he looks at her and sees her expression he gets sacred. Determined to go on he asks, "Can I tell you?"

"Go ahead, tell me," she says, crying.

"I spent the night with Suzie." She begins to cry more loudly. "It was nothing to write home about, but it happened."

Carol looks up at him. Her eyes full of tears she puts her head against Sloan's shoulder. He tries to pull her into his arms, but she won't let him.

"Why didn't you tell me before?" she pleads.

"Even though we had agreed that we would be free to see other people, I knew it would bother you. I know it would have bothered me. I felt guilty and I told myself that we both probably slept with other people during that time, and I felt then that I didn't want to hear about your other lovers. I figured you would feel the same.

"I'm so happy to find out that I'm the only man in your life. You're the only woman I've ever loved and that's the truth, Carol. When you said before that neither of us had ever been with anyone, I felt so bad. I didn't want to lie to you when you were being so loving with me. I didn't want to confuse you and

I decided that you deserve the whole truth. Now that you know I don't have to worry about hiding anything."

Carol was very upset. She said she was not so much upset with the actual deed but with the idea that he had been keeping a secret from her for so long. She felt foolish to think that she had been under a false impression about her husband, the closest person in her life. What hurt Carol more than Sloan's one night stand was the loss of trust.

That night, they held each other tighter than ever. It was a night to remember and it went a long way to help Carol get over her hurt feelings. Later, she even felt flattered that Sloan had preferred her over the universally sought-after Suzie. She understood why he had not told her and decided that, though it was hard to accept at first, she could live with this new information. In the future, when she momentarily found herself wondering if Sloan might be keeping any secrets from her, she was reassured by the thought that if he could tell her about that night, he would probably never lie to her about anything. She felt profoundly safe with him.

People will vehemently argue that this kind of honesty is unnecessary or worse an act of irresponsible, sadistic cruelty. They may argue further that a person in Sloan's position, having made a hurtful mistake should bear the burden of legitimate remorse and keep the painful information away from his wife.

These arguments ignore some important facts. They ignore the damaging effect of even the smallest lie; how it can proliferate into further and bigger lies and how keeping secrets from a partner undermines the intuitive and empathic process between them. Most important it ignores the far greater pain that people feel when they find out that they have been repeatedly lied to over a long time. Imagine how Carol would feel if after five or six years of occasionally meeting Susan Green socially, she found out, through a casual remark by Susan's husband that Sloan and Susan had been lovers.

• **Housekeeping required:** A relationship is only as good as its dialogue. Put time aside for emotional housekeeping. Tell each other about your suspicions, hunches or paranoid fantasies. Listen carefully. Take the opportunity to apologize for hurts. And most of all, find time to give each other strokes.

Don't take care of emotional business during television commercials or when you are too tired to talk about them. Set aside quality time for conversation. Addressing emotional issues during a walk is a recommendation I frequently make. Another possibility is to have regular dates on which you air emotional issues.

• **Review, review, review . . . :** Make sure that you review agreements regularly. In this era of rapid change, agreements that made sense six months ago may no longer make sense.

Talk frequently about issues like money and time, especially where and how each of them should be spent.

Just because you have done things a certain way for a long time doesn't mean that is acceptable to your partner. This is especially true when it comes to sex, which can become routine and acceptable to one person and not acceptable to the other.

• **Be flexible:** Be willing to change your agreements, even after you have negotiated them extensively. Accept change and new points of view. After all, the goal is for both of you to work together in cooperation and produce feelings of affection and hope rather than resentment and despair.

Bill and Hillary are both very busy people. They have no children and are very hard-working. When they finally get together in the evenings they have dinner and barely have enough energy for some chores and a little television in bed. They cuddle while watching TV and usually fall asleep before the set turns itself off. Without talking about it they seem to have agreed to avoid difficult emotional issues. Hillary has been feeling that she is not getting enough intimate discussion time to process some of the problems they have been sweeping under the rug.

One morning as they are getting ready to go to work, Hillary suggests that they take Saturday morning off, drive to the hiking trail and talk over some subjects. Bill balks at first because he has a golf date, but Hillary insists and he eventually agrees.

Next Saturday as they start on their hike Hillary says, "I'm worried that we are drifting apart. Even though we seem to get along and love each other, I am afraid that things are building up between us that feel bad, to me anyway."

"Well, I am feeling okay about things," Bill says. "Is there something you are unhappy about?"

"See, that could be a problem right there. You don't seem to notice that we have these little disagreements which usually end up in one of us, mostly me, going along with you in order to avoid trouble. I keep thinking I am too tired or we'll deal with it tomorrow or that maybe I am being petty but I'm beginning to feel bad . . ."

Bill interrupted, "I realize we are having these little problems but I thought we were dealing with them as we go. I feel okay about them."

"Maybe that is the first problem to talk about, because I am *not* feeling so good. When you say that you think that these problems are being solved . . . Can I tell you how I feel?" Bill nods.

"Actually I feel very angry."

Bill nods again, but he is shaken.

Hillary goes on. "Can I tell you what I am guessing? I suspect that when we disagree you don't realize that most of the time I am going along with you just to keep a good feeling going."

Bill, after thinking, says "I think you are probably right, although I am not sure it's that extreme. But I know I have always taken your easygoing nature somewhat for granted. We've talked about that before, and I am sorry."

For the next hour Hillary recalled a number of incidents where somehow things had gone Bill's way. Some of the incidents were admittedly very unimportant, like the fact that on a crowded sidewalk Bill always walks ahead, or that he almost always drives when they are together, or that he won't make suggestions about restaurants when they go out, or that he is often distracted when they speak. But all of this is building some anger in Hillary. He points out that she goes along so he didn't realize she was upset. She agrees, but says that she is often just too worn out to struggle through talking these things out, and that she would like him to be more aware of these subtle tensions between them.

After some conversation it seemed that the most serious problem was that they didn't have enough time with each other to make Hillary happy. Bill seemed content to sit together and watch TV, sleep together, make love in the mornings or on weekends, and have a few meals out, and for a while Hillary was okay with this too.

But she was beginning to dislike the way sex had become more and more business-like. Even though they had agreed that sex in the mornings would be the best time for both of them, she was beginning to resent its clock-like regularity.

"I don't want to have sex in the mornings anymore," she blurted out.

"Well, when then? You say yourself that we are too tired in the evenings, we are both morning people . . ."

"Well, I guess I want us to take time in the evenings, take a whole evening off after dinner, go out for a drink, talk, get reacquainted with each other's changing lives."

Bill was alarmed by this proposal. He had been happy with their arrangements and he feared that this would take too much time out of their precisely timed lives. He hesitated, and Hillary felt irritated. Their tempers flared and just as they were about to change the subject, Hillary said, "See, this is the way it always goes. We don't deal with our disagreements, and if I let this go we would be back where we started. Let's stay with this please."

They talked for another hour and arrived at some new decisions. Bill realized he hadn't been making his wife a priority. He was willing to try Hillary's unsettling proposal. They also agreed to have one of these "housekeeping walks" once a month.

In the end things did not go exactly as planned. Bill still set certain routines with Hillary, but they did take off one evening a week, television-free, to just be with each other and make love. Their walks sometimes only happened every three months. But all in all this discussion had a very beneficial effect. They reviewed their agreements in a flexible way and they established a way for their relationship to continue on an emotionally literate basis.

EMOTIONAL LITERACY AND CHILDREN

Emotional Literacy is best developed in childhood, when information is learned by example.

Learning skills when you are young, while that window of opportunity is open, is very different from learning them after the window is closed. Reading, for example, is easily learned in our youth. Yet an illiterate adult can have a terrible time learning to read. The same is true of other skills, such as playing sports, learning foreign languages, music, and, yes, Emotional Literacy.

It is during this critical learning period that children establish their various attitudes. They begin to visualize themselves as good or bad, skillful or clumsy, happy or unhappy. They may even think of themselves as fantasy characters. Some children, for instance, will identify with Snow White or one of the Seven Dwarfs. Others will see themselves as Superman or Lois Lane, the Pied Piper or Little Red Riding Hood, even Jesus Christ or the Devil.

They will also adopt the emotional habits that fit their view of themselves: grumpy, sweet, imperturbable, impatient, scheming, saintly, wicked. And once children start acting a certain way, they will be seen by others in that way and will get labeled bad or good, happy or unhappy.

For the most part, these emotional patterns are learned from parents and others around them. Once adopted, these habits become patterns or scripts about what life is and what it will be like. These scripts can last a lifetime unless something is done to change them.

- The child that is habitually sad and afraid may become an adult who is depressed and suicidal.

- The child that learns to supress his tears may become hard-hearted.

- The child that can't control her tantrums may be prone to addictive behaviors as an adult.

The Wrong Way and the Right Way. As an example of how emotional patterns are established by parents, let's look at a typical household "minitragedy" and two ways it might be handled by parents. First, the emotionally *illiterate* way of handling this crisis:

Matthew, a five-year-old, has just fallen from a chair while trying to sneak some cookies. He is crying loudly. Not only does his knee hurt from where he struck it on the floor, but he is humiliated to be caught raiding the cookie jar. He feels hurt, guilty, and frightened at the same time.

His father reaches the kitchen and realizes what his son has been doing. He becomes angry.

"What happened? Did you hurt yourself?" the father asks angrily. "Stop crying!"

How is Matthew to interpret this? Is he supposed to stop feeling pain? How about his fear and guilt? Is he supposed to keep feeling these things but not cry? In confusion, he screams louder.

If his father is emotionally literate, he would let well enough alone. Instead, he sees this as an opportunity to teach Matthew a lesson about life.

"Come on Matthew, stop being such a crybaby," he says. "You're worse than your sister."

Now Matthew gets the idea that crying is bad, that he is somehow "worse than his sister." Maybe he gets the idea that girls can cry but boys cannot, a notion that bothers him. He tries to suppress his crying but he can't. He is just too fearful of his father's disapproval.

Suppose now that his father becomes even more upset and decides to continue his lesson.

"Matthew, that's enough! You know better than this," he declares. "You are acting like a sissy. What were you doing on the kitchen counter anyway?"

Matthew has heard about sissies and boys who act like girls from the other kids at school. He feels very guilty about getting caught being a bad boy. Now he decides to stop crying. He clenches his teeth together and quiets down.

"That's a good boy," says his father.

Many parents feel that it is not proper masculine behavior for boys to cry. Boys who are raised not to cry become grown men who are ashamed to cry. When such a man becomes sad enough to cry, he will hide it by lying about how he feels.

Eventually, he will become so unaware of his own sadness that he will deny it even to himself. He will deny other feelings of vulnerability too, such as shame or longing. At that point he will only recognize the strongest of his emotions, such as furious anger or mad love.

Girls are treated differently. When they cry it is considered sweet or touching. Almost never are girls made to feel that it is not feminine or ladylike to cry.

This may be one reason why women are generally more emotional than men.

A Better Approach. Now let's look at a more emotionally literate response to the cookie incident. After Matthew falls from the chair and hits his knee, his father might pick him up and say: "Boy are you upset. Did you hurt yourself?"

Instead of answering, Matthew lets out a loud scream. He is feeling physical hurt from the fall and guilt from getting caught stealing a cookie.

"Sounds like you are mad at me," says his father, wiping away his son's tears.

"Yeaaaa," says Matthew.

"Why? I'm trying to help you here," says his father. "Can I kiss your booboo?"

He rocks Matthew until the boy begins to calm down.

"Were you trying to get some cookies?"

Matthew begins to cry again.

"Are you feeling guilty? Are you worried I'll get mad?"

Matthew doesn't answer but he is quieting down.

"Well, you know I don't like you to eat so many sweets between meals, but I'm sorry you hurt yourself," says Father. "Next time don't try to get any cookies on your own, okay?"

Instead of trying to stop Matthew's crying, he has helped him understand why he was so upset. He has shown empathy while giving his son the physical strokes of hugs and kisses.

After Matthew calms down, his father will have a conversation with him about what happened, how he felt, and how to avoid these melodramas in the future.

As Matthew grows up, he will have learned that his feelings are valued and that he can safely express them.

EQ Guidelines for Children. Children can begin to learn Emotional Literacy as soon as you show it to them. Eventually you can talk to them about their feelings, usually as soon as they can form a sentence. At about the age of two or three, children begin to feel guilt and are able to empathize with others so they can apologize for the hurt they caused.

The same rules of cooperation that apply to adult relationships should be applied to those between children and adults. Equality, honesty, and the avoidance of power plays are just as important with children, though they may need to be customized to fit the situation. That usually means that you should give children as much power as possible and be as open as you can, avoiding lies in every way possible.

Here are some guidelines that will teach your child Emotional Literacy:

• **Keep the heart open:** Kiss and hug your children often and tell them that you love them. Like all of us, they crave and enjoy affection. If you show them love through physical strokes when they are young, they will be openhearted as they grow up.

• **Don't power play your children:** Never hit your children. By using power plays to get what you want from children, they will learn to be motivated by fear and control. If you do power play your children (as we all do at one time or another) make sure to apologize and explain how you felt. Offer to not do that kind of thing again. Then, with the child and perhaps other family members, work out a better method of getting them to mind you.

Three year old Sarah is fond of pushing buttons and turning dials wherever she can find them. Many times she has turned off FAX machines, readjusted the settings on stereos and TVs, made redial phone calls, and lately has been seen wanting to turn on the gas stove. Her mother, Jane, is very frightened of a gas leak and has told Sarah "No!" many times but Sarah seems to be devilishly focused on doing just that. One time Jane surprised Sarah when she was turning a gas knob. Jane lost control. Yelling at her, she gave Sarah a strong whack on her bottom. Sarah was petrified, and screamed and cried loudly for a few minutes. After Sarah calmed down the following conversation took place:

"Sarah are you still upset?"

Sarah nods.

"Well, I got very angry and I am sorry I hit you. You are not allowed to play with the stove."

"Yes I am."

"No, you are not. The stove is hot and it will burn you. If you do it again, you'll go to time out."

"No I won't, mama."

"Well if you promise to stop pushing and turning buttons I promise not to scare you any more. Do you promise to stop?" Sarah nods imperceptibly.

"Is that a yes?" Sarah nods again.

"Okay if you promise, I won't yell at you again, and you won't go to time out. And I am sorry I scared you."

Sarah starts crying again, and hugs her mother, who hugs her back. "It's okay, honey, I love you, you are a good girl."

Be sensitive to what children want, regardless of how silly it might seem. Listen empathically to them. Try to be understanding when they don't want something because it scares them, embarrasses them, or offends their sense of esthetics or taste. Be flexible when making demands.

• **Be honest:** Being truthful with your children is important, second only to not abusing them with power plays. Explain to them how you feel and what you want from them. Never tell them bald-faced lies and keep your lies of omission to a minimum, making sure to be truthful as soon as possible. If you want them to be truthful, you must first be truthful with them. After all, children sense when secrets are kept from them and will learn to keep secrets from you.

If you have been honest with your children you should assume that they will be truthful with you. Given how commonplace lying is, however, you should look out for lies from children as vigilantly as you eventually will have to look out for drug use. Sooner or later your child will tell a major lie and I believe that to be an extremely important opportunity to practice what you have learned here.

Sally has just come home from school and has gone to her room. She is staying in there longer than usual. Checking, you find her in her room reading.

"Hi Sally. Back from school?" She looks up and seems to be covering what she is reading with a book.

"What are you reading?"

"Nothing."

"It looks like a magazine."

"I said, *nothing*."

By now, you can tell something is fishy. You remind yourself to stay calm, in your Adult.

"It is a magazine, isn't it?"

"Yeah, Mom." She says morosely.

"Whose is it?"

"Kathy's, she lent it to me." By now she looks scared. Meanwhile you have gone over to Sally and picked up the magazine.

"This seems brand new to me. Where did you get it?"

"I told you!" You sit down next to her, look at her averted eyes, and as kindly as possible, speaking from the heart you say:

"Sally are you telling me the truth? Please don't lie to me. You know how I feel about lying. However you got this is not as important to me as you telling the truth. Just tell me and we'll work it out."

"I bought it."

"Oh good, I was afraid that maybe you stole it. I know some kids think it's cool to steal from 7–Eleven."

"Mother, I wouldn't steal. You know that!"

"Good. So how did you get the money to buy it? Tell the truth."

Sally is clearly upset. She looks down. She clams up. You wait. After a few minutes of silence she says:

"I took the money from your wallet."

"Sally, did you really?"

"Yes."

Silence again. You search your feelings. You are scared by what Sally has done and you are sad that she lied to you. You are angry because she has been rebellious lately. You want to tell her that taking money from you is just as bad as stealing from 7-Eleven. Time for an action/feeling statement.

"Sally, can I tell you how I feel about this?"

Sally nods.

Keeping a loving tone, from the heart you say: "When you take money from my wallet to buy a magazine, and then try to lie about it to me, it makes me feel scared and very sad and also angry. Can you understand that?"

She is listening and agrees. You now have an opportunity to find out why she feels she had to steal to buy a trashy magazine. She tells you that you would not buy it for her or let her use her allowance. She tells you the magazine has interesting stories in it. You pick one up and look at the table of contents. Definitely junk.

"Well, Sally, I definitely don't like it, but on the other hand I realize that I can't stop you from being interested in it. But you are not allowed to take money from my wallet and I would like you to apologize for that. More important, I want you to agree not to lie to me. Your lying is what scares me and makes me sad. Because if you start lying we won't be able to talk the way we are used to. And that would be too bad, don't you think?" Sally agrees.

Make truthfulness between you and your child the most important bond between you.

• **Let go of control:** Give your children power by letting them take charge in games. Wrestle with them, let them hit you lightly in play, pretend to cry or get sad. This kind of behavior shows them that you are not always in control.

By the same token, tell them about your feelings. If they want to know why you feel the way you do, explain it to them in short and simple sentences.

• **Understand your children's demons:** Be aware of your children's fears and accept them. Learn to recognize when they are afraid and why. Talk about their fears, validate them, and help avoid them. If you are out of control with your own emotions, shield them from this experience, since it can frighten them badly.

• **Encourage emotionally literate media:** Read emotionally literate books to your children. Take them to emotionally literate films and plays. Avoid stories containing a lot of violence and cruelty, unless they make a clear moral statement about anger and how to deal with it in a good way. The same is true of love and sex: Make sure the message is emotionally literate. Read them *The Warm Fuzzy Tale,* about "warm fuzzies" and "cold pricklies."

179

- **Teach emotional self-defense:** Teach children how to defend their boundaries and reject behavior they don't want by saying, "I don't like that," or "Please stop it," or "Leave me alone."

These are all acceptable and effective ways of deflecting unwanted behavior. Role play such situations and teach them how to respond to different scenarios.

- **Be patient:** Educating children takes time, but once they've learned, the lesson will stick. Repeat your lessons over and over in a consistent manner and be sure to live what you preach. Remember: An apple doesn't fall far from the tree.

EQ IN THE WORKPLACE

Introducing Emotional Literacy in the workplace is a subject worthy of a whole book. I can only hope to give some basic hints here.

Emotional literacy is best learned when we have an agreement with people to conduct a cooperative relationship that is free of power plays and where rescues and lies are consciously avoided.

Work environments are usually just the opposite. It is in the workplace that we are most likely to find power plays and wholesale lying and keeping of secrets. In fact, some work settings encourage emotionally illiterate behavior. It is not uncommon to hear about managers who threaten workers with losing their jobs if they step out of line, or to hear about workers who are sexually harassed. Even though workers may have the law on their side, the law has no teeth without an expensive lawyer and most workers have little recourse but to submit. Secrets about salaries, promotions, firings, and plant closings are routine.

Most workplace power plays are not so overt, however. Subtle power plays abound, not just from bosses and management but among workers. Pecking orders develop and with them come subtle insults, secrets, gossip, lies, and hurtful humor.

Even though most people realize what is going on, there is

no agreement to stop these actions or to prevent them. Consequently, the workplace can be a minefield of emotionally illiterate, toxic transactions.

How can a person create an emotionally literate workplace? It isn't easy. Even in work environments known for easygoing friendliness, a great deal of emotional illiteracy can be taking place. Basically, you want to displace an emotionally illiterate culture and try to establish a different one, in which power plays are not used and emotions are considered worthy of attention.

You can start the process of change by finding at least one person inside the organization who has the same interest in Emotional Literacy as you do. Then find others. You can build interest by showing this book to people or by posting a copy of the Emotional Literacy Commandments, which can be found at the end of this chapter.

Everything I have tried to teach in this book can be tried in the workplace, though it may be far more difficult. Emotional Literacy at work is more risky because it has to be practiced without a cooperative contract to protect you from power plays, lies, and rescues. Be prepared for people to refuse to cooperate, or even have a hostile reaction.

For instance, Mark, a coworker on your team, regularly makes comments about your colorful ties. You suspect that he feels competitive with you because you have some advanced computer skills that he lacks. In any case, you want to tell him that the way he keeps kidding you about your choice of ties makes you angry. You wind up feeling depressed and hopeless about working with him. You realize that you have contributed to the problem by going along with the joke so far, but you would like him to stop.

All the basic rules apply: you should obtain permission but in this case, because people are not used to being asked, and if asked may agree without thinking, you must be extra careful to have "informed consent" from him instead of just agreement.

"Hey, Mark, when you have a minute I'd like to pick a bone with you. Is that okay?"

Mark: (perplexed) "Yeh, sure."

"Well it's sort of a complaint, are you sure you want to hear it?"

Mark: (looking genuinely alarmed) "What did I do wrong?"

"It's not that bad, but I want to make sure that you want to hear."

Mark: "Well okay. How about now?"

"Now? Later might be better, when we have a little time."

"How about after work?"

"That's good. Don't worry about it, it's just something that has been troubling me. But I'm sure we'll work it out just fine ... Let's meet at the Hut."

You can see that what would take one transaction in a contractual, cooperative relationship can take several minutes of conversation in the real world. And of course it may not work out as neatly as I suggest.

But that does not mean that it can't be done. In all probability, given a skillful, open-hearted approach, Mark will be primed and ready to hear your feedback and you'll be able to establish an understanding so that he will stop kidding you about your clothes.

You can give strokes, ask for strokes, accept and reject strokes just as I have explained, but again every one of these transactions will require more preparation, be more complicated and lengthy, and have more risk of backfiring. You can deliver action/feeling statements and intuitive hunches and you can hope that you will get an emotionally literate response. If not you can try to extract a good response but that may be far more difficult.

For instance, you might feel that you have worked long and hard on a project for your boss and haven't gotten enough praise for it. You are feeling bad about yourself and you need strokes. Instead of just asking for permission and then simply asking for some strokes from your boss you have to approach the matter much more diplomatically.

"Helen, do you have a minute? I would like to ask you something."

"I'm busy now."

Helen is not a woman of many words. You sense that she likes you, but this will not be easy. "How about later?" you ask.

"Okay," she says without looking up from her work. Not unfriendly, just busy.

"What's a convenient time for you?"

"I'll call you in your office as soon as I'm done here. About a half an hour."

Great. Now comes the hard part.

Helen calls you in your office. "You wanted to talk?"

You are scared, your mouth is dry and at this point it feels safer to drop the matter, but you are determined and you press on.

"Yes, can I come over to your office?"

"You don't want to speak on the phone?"

"I would rather speak face to face if you don't mind." There is a split second of silence. Helen is getting the idea that this conversation is special. "Okay, come right over."

Seconds later when you get to Helen's office she looks up from her desk and beckons you in. She is clearly curious. She signals you to sit down.

"So what do you have on your mind?"

"Helen, I am a bit nervous doing this, but I wanted to ask you a question. May I?"

"Sure, go ahead."

"You know that we just finished a very large project and that I worked long and hard hours on it."

"Yes."

"Well, I am not clear on whether you liked the job I did."

"I thought I told you that I appreciated how hard you worked on it, didn't I?"

"Yes, you did but you know I don't get any feeling that you appreciated anything but how hard I worked. I mean working hard is no guarantee of quality. Did you find the work I did particularly good?"

"Yes of course, that goes without saying."

"If you don't mind, if there is something specific you can say about it I would really appreciate hearing it. I am feeling underappreciated these days, not particularly by you, but in general. Would you mind?"

"Actually I thought the work was quite exceptional, really."

"I hate to press you on this, but could you say how so?"

"It was very creative and also very precise. I thought you knew that."

"I guess I do, but it's good to hear it from you. Thanks for indulging me. I hope this wasn't a bother for you . . ."

"Not at all, I am sorry that you have been feeling under-appreciated. I am very glad that you are working for me."

Of course this is a very positive scenario. Helen could have chided you for fishing for strokes or being childish. Or she could have refused to elaborate on her praise. In an emotionally illiterate environment that would not be too unusual. If this had happened you would have had to discreetly excuse yourself and leave the matter there, or use the information to improve your work. But most people even in emotionally illiterate situations want to be good to others, and the likely outcome in most of these situations will be positive.

PRACTICE WHAT YOU PREACH

If you are in a position to supervise people then you will be able to put some of these principles into practice. Discreetly ask permission whenever you bring up emotionally loaded material. You can give strokes and ask for strokes. You can gladly accept strokes you want and politely reject strokes you don't want. Even give yourself strokes.

Practice telling people how their actions make you feel and get them to hear you without being defensive. Listen to their feelings.

State your intuitive hunches and attempt to extract validation for them. If you do this in an open-hearted and flexible manner most people will be receptive, since you are in a position to protect them from power plays. As the boss, however, you will be responsible to make sure that you are not forcing these ideas on powerless and unwilling people who have to go along with you. As an example, let's assume that you are a line supervisor in a factory with 25 workers under you. You enjoy being friendly with your workers and you like to be treated in a friendly way.

One of your best workers seems to be unhappy at work. She does not greet you in her usual friendly fashion and she seems withdrawn from other workers. Your intuition tells you that there is something wrong and you decide to investigate in an emotionally literate fashion.

You approach Paula on her break. "How are you today, Paula?"

"Fine."

"May I ask you a question?"

She nods.

You must make sure that Paula is genuinely willing. "Are you sure? I don't want to intrude." The tone of your voice will have everything to do with her feeling that she has a choice. You must really feel and mean that she is free to decline your question.

Let's say you gain her permission. "Sure."

"Well, I have noticed that you seem quiet. I have a hunch that something is upsetting you."

"Oh no, everything is okay," she says unconvincingly.

Normally, in a cooperative situation, it would be perfectly permissible to insist on more of an answer. But in this instance, if you insist you could be abusing your power; she may not want to tell you what's wrong or talk to you at all.

"Well, I'm glad. Can I tell you how I feel?" Again, she nods.

"When you are so quiet I get worried that something is wrong. And I would be sad if there is something I could help with, and you didn't ask."

She looks at you dubiously.

"Do you believe me?"

She nods again.

"Okay, well please keep in mind that I am here to be helpful if I can. Let me know if there is anything you want me to do."

With that you best leave the situation alone. You may feel sad or even angered by Paula's unwillingness to talk to you. You may be mistaken that there is anything wrong. In any case you have laid a foundation for future emotionally literate conversations with Paula. If you behave in this manner reliably you will acquire a good reputation with your workers and hopefully with your superiors. You may actually be able to demonstrate that this approach improves morale and productivity with your workers and even succeed in having other supervisors try it.

For a person in a position of power, apologizing is a good way of demonstrating that you really mean to be emotionally literate. You will obviously make mistakes, and in the traditional workplace these mistakes are usually not acknowledged. It will be truly impressive to your workers if you seem cognizant of your errors, admit them, and apologize and make amends to those you may have affected badly with them.

START AN EMOTIONAL LITERACY STUDY AND SUPPORT GROUP

Notice who in your workplace is able to accept and even enjoy the steps of this program and stroke them for it. They are the ones who will most likely be interested in joining a support group.

The ideal size of such a support group is eight to twelve people. With a group this size you can begin to institute real change. For example, a lunchtime group of this size would have a noticeable presence in most organizations and would certainly grow. You could even organize a training weekend. Possibly, the group could convince your boss to finance a weekend retreat by showing him how it would improve the mood and productivity of the workplace.

Why would these efforts create a positive transformation? Again most people, whether they believe in emotional literacy training or not, have a desire for good strokes and a need to express how they feel safely. In an environment where they give and receive all that emotional literacy training promises, they will be happier and more productive people.

TEN COMMANDMENTS OF EMOTIONAL LITERACY

1. **Thou shalt not power play.** Ask instead for what you want until you get it.
2. **Thou shalt not allow yourself to be power played.** Don't do anything you are not willing to do of your own free will.
3. **Thou shalt not lie by omission or commission.** Except where your safety or the safety of others is concerned, avoid lying.
4. **Thou shalt stand up for how you feel and what you want.** If you don't, it is not likely that anyone else will.
5. **Thou shalt respect the feelings and wishes of others.** That does not mean you have to submit to them.
6. **Thou shalt look for the validity in the ideas of others.** There is more than one way to look at things.
7. **Thou shalt apologize and make amends for your mistakes.** Nothing will allow you to grow faster.
8. **Thou shalt want to forgive others for their mistakes.** Do unto others as you would have them do unto you.
9. **Thou shalt not accept false apologies.** They are worth less than no apologies at all.
10. **Thou shalt follow these commandments according to your best judgment.** After all, they are not written in stone.

8

THE EMOTIONAL WARRIOR

In this book I have taught you a series of powerful techniques to increase your Emotional Literacy. These techniques will help you improve your relationships in all areas of your life. They will also increase your level of personal power.

Many people have been so impressed by the results of emotional literacy training that they want to involve their friends, family, and lovers with these ideas. Some even believe that these ideas should become part of a moral code.

Over the years I have met a number of people who have seen emotional literacy training as a tool for social change and want to apply it beyond their own personal lives. These people belong in a worldwide team of activists that I call Emotional Warriors.

THE ANCIENT REGIME

People throughout history have been dominated by leaders who have used any method available to stay in control. These methods can be physical or psychological, but they are always backed by intimidating threats of violence. In this system of domination, people are placed on a pyramid of power, one-up to some and one-down to others with every level controlling the level below. Secrets and the control of information are an important method of keeping power.

In the military, a classic example of a control power culture, everyone lower down has someone he or she has to salute and obey. In this system, insubordination is severely punished, and information is closely held on a "need to know" basis.

In most corporations, the employees pay homage to the bosses who send the memos and downsize the corporation. Often the workers don't know their boss's intentions, or are purposely misled.

These systems of domination didn't come about by accident. They are part of the basic structure in our society known as patriarchy.

In classic patriarchy, a father heads a clan or tribe, and his authority is passed down through the male line. In today's patriarchies, the father figure passes power down according to his whim—usually to one or more of his male followers, but sometimes, also, to carefully selected women.

The system is kept in place by domination, whether in government, the workplace, or in families.

All this domination is exercised through person-to-person transactions or power plays. The sergeant who "writes up" a soldier for having a sloppy uniform, the boss who expects a greeting from his secretary but who doesn't bother to respond, the father who smiles dismissively whenever his young daughter wants to be heard—these are all dominating power transactions.

UNDERSTANDING CONTROL POWER

We hardly notice how domination works, because we are immersed in it from birth.

The value of Transactional Analysis as a tool to understand relationships can be seen clearly here. With it, you can analyze power relations, examine them, and once you understand them, figure out how to avoid them in yourself and others.

After spending our childhood at the mercy of other people's whims, we accept as natural that we should be either victimizers or victims one up or one down, leader or follower, dominator or dominated. The slapped child becomes the parent who slaps, the child who is dominated and controlled becomes the parent who dominates and controls. We accept abuse and control power as the way of the world.

If we want to fight unreasonable control and power abuse effectively, we need to fully understand how power plays work.

The chart on the opposite page shows you four ways in which control power is used:

CRUDE

I • __Crude, Physical__	II • __Crude, Psychological__
murder	insults
rape	menacing tones
imprisonment	interrupting
torture	sulking
besting	ignoring
beating	blatant lying
shoving	
banging doors	
screaming	

PHYSICAL · PSYCHOLOGICAL

III • __Subtle, Physical__	IV • __Subtle, Psychological__
touching	false logic
looming	sarcastic humor
space invasion	discounting
leading by the arm	"attitude"
making someone stand or sit	lies of omission
	advertising, propaganda

SUBTLE

There are two main forms of control power: physical and psychological. Each can be expressed either subtly or crudely. There are four types of power plays: crude physical, subtle physical, crude psychological, and subtle psychological. A power play is a transaction in which one person tries to force another person to do something against his or her will.

Crude physical power plays are obvious to the naked eye and include hitting, shoving, throwing things, banging doors, or worse, kidnapping, torture, rape and murder.

Subtle physical power plays are not as easily visible, although you may become aware that you are being power-played after a while. Still, you may have no idea how power plays work or how to stop them.

They include such things as towering over people or standing close to them so that you invade their personal space, leading them by the elbow or hand or walking ahead of them, making people stand or sit or blocking their path. These power plays are often used by men on women, who accept them as a matter of normal male behavior.

Psychological power plays work because people are trained to obey from early childhood; without using physical force I can intimidate you with threats or with the tone of my voice. I can push you to action by making you feel guilty. I can seduce you with a smile or a promise, or persuade you that what I want is the right thing to do. I can trick you, con you, or sell you a lie. If I can overcome your resistance without using physical force, I have used a psychological power play. Psychological power plays are all around us in daily life. Some are crude, some are subtle.

Crude psychological power plays include menacing tones and looks, insults, bald-faced lies, and blatant sulking. Also: interrupting, ignoring, making faces, rolling your eyes, tapping your fingers, and humming while others talk.

Subtle psychological power plays include clever lies, lies of omission, subtle sulking, sarcastic humor, gossip, false logic, ignoring what people say, and at a mass level, advertising and propaganda.

Examples of physical power abuse are more shocking than those of psychological abuse, and they are less widespread. Even in the most violent environments, such as prisons or battlefields, people do not suffer primarily from direct physical oppression. Instead, their minds are controlled by the threat of violence. This is especially true in homes where women and children are physically abused and battered.

AVENUES TO POWER

There are two widely different ways of becoming powerful in this world: power plays and power literacy.

The first requires being a person with no feeling for others and therefore no limits to his grasping needs. A chronic power player feels little empathy for others; such people need to be cold to their victims' pain and will do whatever is necessary to keep control.

Power Literacy. I have been speaking and teaching about an important source of personal power in this book, the power of Emotional Literacy. To become an emotional warrior, however, you need "power literacy" in addition to Emotional Literacy. In other words, you need to understand how power operates, how it is accumulated, how to take power, how to share it, and, at times, how to give it up.

The problem is that in a domination-based system such as ours, power is often inaccurately defined as "the capacity to control other people."

Unfortunately, most thinking about power runs along these lines. Power theorists ignore other important forms of power, such as the power of communication, knowledge, or love.

To be passionate, centered, or spiritually aware is to be powerful. There is no better example of this type of power than Nelson Mandela, who completely changed the political direction of South Africa from his prison cell. And what historical figure was more powerful than Jesus of Nazareth? He was a poor carpenter who changed the world with his message of love.

Knowledge is another example of power that rivals control. That is why authoritarian governments have always done what they could to prevent people from being educated or from gathering freely to learn from each other.

One reason the totalitarian governments of Eastern Europe collapsed was that improved communications across their borders destroyed their ability to control the flow of information and neutralized their propaganda. This is another example of how control is ultimately an unstable approach to power.

Many people renounce power because they see it used only for dominance or control. They think that to be powerful, you can't love people and be truly concerned about their fate. Because of this, rejecting power is seen as a good and necessary thing.

But equating powerlessness with virtue is a form of power illiteracy. In fact, personal power is the capacity to make things happen. People should strive to be as powerful as they can be, without taking power away from others.

THE MANY FACES OF PERSONAL POWER

Personal power goes far beyond being able to manipulate or control people.

You have power when you can bring about what you seek and prevent what you don't want. On the other hand you are powerless when you can't bring about what you want; or can't stop things you wish to avoid.

The president of a corporation who manipulates politicians and workers may be powerless to get the love of his wife and family. All his control power is useless to get him a happy personal life.

We are powerless when we can't control what we eat or drink, or put in our bodies, when we can't sleep or stay awake, when we can't think clearly or control our emotions. We are especially powerless, and feel this keenly, when we can't curb other people's controlling and oppressive behavior.

If you can muster the energy and skills to cope with these problems, your life will likely develop satisfactorily. If you can't, your life will be joyless and filled with turmoil and depression, psychosis, and addiction.

The Internal Enemy. One important reason why we become powerless is that we have an internal enemy that constantly weakens us from within. When people are systematically abused, most of them will, in time, abuse other people and themselves. In this way, they become their own and each other's abusers, prison guards, and torturers.

A good example of this is the Nazi concentration camps where the Jewish capos, appointed by the wardens to guard their fellow Jews, adopted their captors' cruel ways. Examples abound in which oppressed people turned on each other and treated each other as viciously as their oppressors did.

But this process also works when people are subjected to subtle psychological abuse. Such abuse is hidden and unacknowledged and tends to be forgotten. But it is taken in and eventually becomes the internal Critical Parent and so remains inside people's minds, keeping them in line and punishing them for every thought or act that breaks its oppressive rules.

When children, introverts, women, people of color, workers, lesbians, gay men, physically handicapped people, and old, poor, or "ugly" folk are mistreated, they can feel so powerless that they come to accept the mistreatment and believe that it is deserved. Eventually, they abuse themselves, physically and psychologically, as they follow the dictates of the Critical Parent in scores of self-destructive, self-loathing ways.

In this way they have absorbed society's patriarchal scheme, which says it is all right for some people to dominate and for others to be beaten down. In fact, patriarchy implies that those who are beaten down are somehow "wrong." It does that by labelling the poor as "lazy," or women as "irrational," or minorities as intellectually and morally inferior.

In this book I have explained how the Critical Parent operates. Self-persecution is the work of the Critical Parent, called variously the "harsh superego," the "Pig Parent," "the Destructive Critic," or the "Enemy." Whatever it is called, it is a voice or an image in the mind saying that the person is bad, stupid, ugly, crazy or doomed—in short, not okay. What's more, that voice is passed down the generations from parents to children, reverberating dreadfully through the minds of whole populations.

In emotional literacy training we have vowed to remove the Critical Parent from our lives, a hard but worthwhile task. But fighting our own Critical Parent is not enough. In fact it is a hopeless task unless we also resist the controlling patriarchial power all around us.

We don't need to fight this battle alone. People everywhere are struggling to run their own lives and are eager to join in the battle for self-determination. To succeed in this struggle we need to develop a new form of personal non-abuse power known as charisma.

SEVEN SOURCES OF POWER

I am now going to show you just what I mean by describing seven sources of nonabusive power. Students of Eastern religions will recognize the origin of these ideas in the ancient theory of the chakras of Kundalini yoga: Earth, Sex, Power, Heart, Throat, Third Eye, and Cosmos.

I call these seven power sources Balance, Passion, Control, Love, Communication, Information, and Transcendance.

No one of these powers should be valued over another. Instead, they should be used together, for each has its own unique capacity to bring about change. When you use them in combination, you will soon see that this rainbow of options is much more powerful than the blunt, often brutal forms of control power that dominate so many of us.

1. Balance: Steady on your feet. Balance or *grounding*, as it is also called, is the capacity to be rooted and comfortable while standing, climbing, walking, or running.

When you have a well-developed capacity for balance, you "know where you stand." Because you know where you stand, you will not be easily pushed out of your physical or personal position. Your body will be firmly planted, and so will your mind.

As with all the power sources, you should try to reach a "happy medium" in regard to balance. If you are deficient in balance, you will be too obedient, easily frightened, and timid. But if you overdevelop balance, you will be stubborn, stony, dense, unmovable, and dull.

Balance is a particularly valuable power source for women. Patriarchy discourages women from attaining a strong sense of physical balance. Women's fashions designed to please men—tight clothes, miniskirts, high heels—interfere with physical stability. So do the requirements of modesty—limited and careful motion—for women of "breeding."

Men, on the other hand, are free to be as physically comfortable as they desire, wear roomy clothing and shoes, and have minimal requirements for grooming and modesty.

In the United States, as women move slowly toward equal status with men, they are casting aside many of the dictates of dress and grooming that have been required for them. As a result, they are feeling more powerful—more rooted, grounded, and balanced.

2. Passion: The heat that keeps you going. The power of passion can invigorate you like nothing else. Passion can create or destroy. Passion brings opposites together, forces confrontation and change.

In the absence of sexual passion, there would be no Romeo and Juliet, few marriages, no unrequited love. But passion is not only sexual. It also fuels missionary zeal, quixotic quests, and revolution.

If your passion is underdeveloped, you will be tepid, boring, and gutless. If your passion boils over, you will explode with unbridled energy.

3. Control: Keeping a firm grip. Control has been badly used but it is an essential form of power. Control allows you to manipulate your environment and the objects, machines, animals, and people in it.

Such control, which is both physical and psychological, also gives you power over yourself. Control is especially important when, in the form of self-discipline, it lets you regulate your other powers, such as passion, information, communication, and your emotions. This control is vital when events around you run amok and threaten your survival. Emotional Literacy is partially a matter of controlling emotions as you need to for a powerful personal approach.

If you lack in control power, you can be victimized by your inner turmoil and become addicted, depressed, sleepless, and slothful. Or you may be victimized by the outer world, becoming unemployed, homeless, battered, persecuted, mentally ill, or sickened by pollution. You will be seen as lacking discipline, unable to control what you feel, say, and do, and what you put in your mouth, up your nose, or into your veins. On the opposite end of the spectrum when obsessed by control you become preoccupied with dominating every situation you are in.

4. Love: Your binding power. Everyone wants to love and to be loved, knowing how good it feels. But few people look beyond love's obvious pleasures to see its power. Fewer yet fully develop that power.

Love is more than just Valentine's Day cards, the thrill that you get when you see your beloved, or the warm hug a mother gives her child. Love has the power to bind people together, enabling them to work tirelessly side by side on the hardest tasks, instilling hope that can propel them out of the most hellish situations—famines, wars, plane wrecks.

If your power of love is underdeveloped, you will be cold, lacking in warmth or empathy for other people, unable to nurture or to be nurtured, unable even to love yourself.

If this power is overdeveloped, you will be a habitual Rescuer, driven to excessive sacrifices for others while neglecting yourself.

Love is at the center of this array of ethical powers. A loving attitude guides the Emotional Warrior. This attitude applies to three elementary realms: Love of self, love of others, and love of truth.

Where Emotional Literacy provides the indispensable tools for a good life, these three qualities provide the vision necessary for a heart-centered approach to living. Let me define these qualities further:

• *Bedrock individuality; love of self.* This means that we stand our ground in defense of our personal uniqueness. Bedrock individuality keeps us firmly focused on what we want and makes us capable of deciding what will contribute or detract from our personal path. Only a passionate love of self will give one the strength to persevere when everyone loses faith in what it is we are doing.

• *Steadfast loyalty; love of others.* By being loyal we are aware of our involvement in the lives of other human beings and equally passionate about others as we are about ourselves. Love of self without love of others is selfish. Love of others without love of self makes us Rescuers who give everything away.

Love of self and others can only be sustained by keeping in touch with our own true feelings and those of others.

• *Conscious truthfulness; love of truth.* Love of self and others cannot be effectively pursued if we ignore truth.

Truthfulness is especially important in the information age, where we can be "well informed," and at the same time under the influence of false and deceitful information.

We must actively participate in "radical truth telling," the refinement of honest communication. Love of truth is the attribute that keeps a person actively involved in pursuing valid information, that is information that reflects the realities of the world.

5. Communication: Your link to others. To reproduce your thoughts and feelings in others, you must use the power of communication. Two operations are involved: sending and receiving, speaking and listening. You need communication to transmit knowledge, to solve problems with others, to build satisfying relationships—in short, to achieve Emotional Literacy.

If you are lacking in communication power, you will be unable to learn much or to enjoy people. If you stress communication too much, you could become a compulsive, careless talker, paying too little attention to what you are saying or its effect on others.

All the forms of power work with each other. A very powerful combination used by great teachers is communication, information, and love. Their communication is inspired by the love of truth and the love of people. They do not browbeat, they do not use control. Therefore, their students are free to compare their teacher's instruction with what they already know, forming their own opinions. Thus they gain personal power.

6. Information: Your antidote to uncertainty. The power of information is that it reduces your uncertainty. When you have information, you can anticipate events and you can make things happen or prevent them from happening.

If you are lacking in the power of information, you suffer from ignorance. If this power is overdeveloped, you tend to rely excessively on science and technology, becoming hyperintellectual and heartless.

Information comes to you in four forms: science, intuition, wisdom and vision.

Science gathers facts methodically, by taking a careful look at things and noting how they work. Science is like a camera taking snapshots of reality. It is a powerful source of certainty.

Intuition grasps the flow of things. It produces "educated guesses" about the way things are. Intuition isn't as exact as science, but it is a powerful guide toward what is probably true. Because of this, intuition is often vital in the early stages of important scientific discoveries. But when we rely too much on intuition, without checking it against reality, we can become paranoid.

Wisdom, or historical perspective, comes from knowledge of past events, either through personal experience or through the study of history. While not exact like science, wisdom can be a powerful tool to help you forecast events.

Vision is the ability to see what lies ahead directly, through dreams and visions.

Ordinarily, our society considers science the only valid source of knowledge; wisdom is for old people, intuition for women, and vision for lunatics. Still, each of these forms of information has validity and can add to your charisma.

Information has been badly misused over the ages. It has been used in the service of control, to wage war, to seize land, and to impose political and religious views.

Today, in the Information Age, the misuse of information comes in the form of disinformation, false advertising, negative political ads and other forms of modern propaganda. They are used to manipulate millions of people through television and other mass media and to persuade people to live certain life styles and buy the products that go with them.

Information in the service of love would be starkly different. It would be used to build people's power—their health through medical and psychological knowledge, their wisdom through education, their relationships through Emotional Literacy.

7. Transcendance: Rising above it all. When viewed as a source of power, Transcendence is the power of detachment, of letting events take their course without getting upset or letting your ego get involved. It lets you find calm and see clearly, in the midst of earthshaking events.

You find transcendance by realizing how insignificant you really are in the universe—how brief life is before you return to cosmic dust, how ephemeral your successes and failures, how relatively unimportant your pains and joys.

Whatever your situation may be, you can deal with it when you see it as a tiny speck in the immensity of time and space.

With this understanding, you will not fear the future or even death because your fundamental place within the universe cannot be disrupted by ordinary events.

The power of transcendence gives you hope and faith that there is a meaning to your life that your limited intelligence can't grasp. With it you can "rise above" a particular situation and trust and feel your power in spite of material conditions.

If your capacity for transcendence is underdeveloped, you will see yourself at the very center of things and cling desperately to your beliefs and desires no matter the cost. You will fail to see the effect that you have on other human beings and the environment, because all that matters to you is you.

If transcendance is overused by you as a method of coping, you will become too detached from earthly matters, so that you will "float away" oblivious of events around you, unwilling and unable to touch the ground.

My knowledge about these sources of power is quite embryonic. I understand some (control, communication) better than others (transcendence, vision). I invite you, dear reader, to add what you know about these subjects by communicating with me by mail or through the web page given at the end of this book.

A SHIFT FOR THE MILLENNIUM

By developing each of the seven sources of power, you can cultivate the Emotional Warrior within yourself.

Right now, our society's fixation on control leaves many people at the mercy of the control hierarchy—corrupt politicians, heartless moguls, cynical advertising executives, and business executives with a chainsaw mentality.

If we were to observe power in Western culture today, we would see a core of control influencing all the other sources of power.

- Transcendance would be distorted into patriarchal religions worshiping wrathful gods and headed by religious leaders who have spiritually sold out for power and money.

- Information would be narrowly limited to the use of science to serve war technology, and to sell goods.

- Communication would be a one-way process to manipulate people.

- Love would be a degraded parody of itself, laden with jealousy and obsession, heralded in popular songs and films but ignored in real life.

- Passion would be reduced to lust and violence.

- Balance would be the exclusive realm of athletic super-heroes.

Our lives don't have to be like this. As Emotional Warriors, we can use all of our love-centered powers to make change happen. We can shift the world away from control and in the direction of love.

You can enlist in this effort by developing your individual power and charisma in its many forms. You need:

- Balance to stand your ground.

- Passion to energize you.

- Control to keep a steady course.

- Communication to effectively interact with others.

- Information to make accurate predictions.

- Transcendance to keep perspective.

- Love to harmonize and give all these capacities a powerful forward thrust.

Emotional literacy training speaks directly to the heart, calling for people everywhere to practice three interconnected virtues: love of self, love of others, and love of truth.

This is the path of the Emotional Warrior.

SUMMARY

The Emotional Warrior

You don't have to go along with a world where human power is expressed through power plays or violence. You can work for a world in which power is expressed through love; of yourself, others and truth.

You can do this by becoming emotionally literate and teaching emotional literacy techniques to others.

To be passionate, balanced, and spiritually aware is to be powerful. There are seven benign sources of power you can draw on: Balance, Passion, Control, Love, Communication, Information, and Transcendance.

Leading with your heart, informed by Emotional Literacy, use these sources of power. Develop your own charisma and while looking out for others, you will become an Emotional Warrior.

9

ONE LAST WORD

Love is a word often used in this book, a word generally overused, easily abused and yet . . . love, I think most would agree, makes the world go 'round. What love is, exactly, is not clear, but certainly it goes beyond the well known passion between lovers or the adoration of our offspring. It is the deep instinct that makes us enjoy being with each other, taking care of one another and doing things together. When we allow it to express itself it helps us survive and prosper.

Of the many things I have said in this book, I want to reemphasize one, and do it in my own voice: Love is at the very center of Emotional Literacy. Any emotional intelligence that we may accumulate apart from the loving emotion is like a paint-by-the-numbers canvas that may look good to the casual gaze but is not the real thing. If you begin by giving and taking strokes you will open up your heart and access the only lasting basis for an emotionally literate life.

Very likely you will wonder how the practice of a few transactional exercises could possibly produce such a powerful source of energy and power. Isn't that a bit of paint-by-the-numbers alchemy to turn psychological lead into gold? I am not promising to *create* a loving heart. What I am assuring you is that these transactions practiced honestly with another willing and sympathetic person will *unleash* that power. Giving and receiving strokes will force open the gates that imprison our hearts. The rest is up to that irresistible power of nature: Love. It may not seem so to some, but Love is ready to come forth and do battle with our dark side, if we will let it and if we can find ways to make it safe and nurture it as it grows.

Eventually, whether or not you develop your Emotional Literacy will depend on a number of factors: Your desire, whether you can find people to practice with, the opportunities afforded you in this cruel world and how successful you are in avoiding its dark side. In these last words I want to make sure, dear reader, that you understand that this book's message has everything to do with Love—of yourself, of others, and of truth.

—Claude Steiner
July 1997
Berkeley, California

NOTES FOR PHILOSOPHERS

With these notes I am following the example set by Eric Berne. In his writings, he provided his readers with the historical and philosophical background for his views. These notes are the result of interviews with Jude Hall about the the philosophical controversies surrounding the issues raised in this book.

Love as a Fundamental Good

The idea of love as a basic good, to be universally pursued with all other human beings, is a markedly Christian notion. It was first espoused in the West by Jesus Christ and in China by Mo Di, a contemporary of Confucius' disciple Mencius.

The most influential critic of Christianity's concept of love is Friedrich Nietzsche. He held that the universal love espoused by Christians is disingenuous, hypocritical, neurotic, and leads to depressive nihilism (what he called passive nihilism) and to the degeneracy of society[1] and the arts. He maintained that the universal love and altruism to which Christians aspire necessitates an egalitarian leveling which prevents society from producing excellence by assigning privilege evenly among all people, when it should go to the especially gifted. These special individuals should be allowed to secure the power they need to achieve their vision. Nietzsche's idols were Napoleon, Julius Caesar, Augustus Caesar, and early Roman emperors, strong men after the fashion of his human ideal, the superman.

While this may sound bizarre to the average reader, Nietzsche (who died in 1900) is considered one of the most influential figures in twentieth century thought, and his critique of the hidden psychological roots of altruism is accepted by thinkers as diverse as Max Horkheimer, Theodore Adorno, and Michael Foucalt. Some aspects of Nietzschian thought have even influenced as egalitarian a thinker as Herbert Marcuse. Thus, as deviant as Nietzsche's ideas may seem to the uninitiated, they cannot be dismissed.

Students of contemporary politics may recognize the traces of the Nietzschian point of view in the theories of conservative politicians today. The belief that social services and government subsidies to help the disadvantaged are undesirable is the permissible manifestation of a far more extreme elitist conviction which permeates the corridors of conservatism throughout the world.

Paradoxically, though the views of this book originate in the teachings about brotherly love of Jesus of Nazareth, they are likely to be classified as secular humanism, anathema to fundamentalist Christians.

Lying and Honesty

The idea that lying is a universal evil was recorded in one of the ten commandments brought down from Mt. Sinai by Moses; "Thou shall not bear false witness." Though it is a fundamental Judeo-Christian dictum, there is very little attention paid to just what, precisely, obeying the rule would imply. When speaking of truth in this book I am applying the well-known criteria followed in the courts, namely that in order not to lie one needs to tell "the whole truth (no lies of omission) and nothing but the truth (no lies of commission.)"

According to this definition, a lie is a conscious act, so that a person cannot lie without being aware of it. The truth is simply the truth as the speaker knows it. In this sense, lying and truth-telling is related to subjective truth and only vaguely related to the abstract and unattainable concept of "the truth." (See notes on The Truth).

St. Augustine was the foremost proponent of absolute truthfulness. He believed that "God forbids all lies."[2] The notion that one should never lie was taken to its political extreme by Immanuel Kant,[3] who argued that it would be a moral crime to lie to a murderer about the whereabouts of a potential victim. Benjamin Constant[4] countered that "no one has the right to a truth that injures others." In this book, while arguing that being truthful is a requirement of Emotional Literacy, I recognize that the imperative of truth-telling is secondary to the imperative of people's safety. Thus any person aspiring to be radically truthful has to keep in mind that truth-telling can, on occasion, be harmful and needs to be evaluated according to circumstances. This may seem to open the door for all manner of lies to preserve people's safety. But there are, in everyday life, very few situations that warrant lying on the basis of safety and certainly no justification whatsoever for the constant dishonesty accepted as normal. Most of the lies people tell have nothing to do with protecting others or oneself from harm, and everything to do with manipulating people to one's advantage, often under the guise of attempting to shield each other from "needless" pain.

According to Dr. Bella de Paulo[5] "everyday lies are part of the fabric of social life," and in a study of people lying she found that people lie in one fifth of their social interactions and that seventy percent of those who lie would tell the lies again.

Sixty percent of the lies were outright deceptions, a tenth of the lies were exaggerations and the rest were subtle lies, often lies of omission.

In her book, *Lying*, Sissela Bok,[6] the acknowledged expert on the issue, classifies all manner of lies and secrets and acknowledges the harm that chronic lying causes us. Yet she does not go as far as to recommend that people should not lie at all, mostly, it seems, because of her apprehension that radical honesty can lend itself to sadistic misuse.

In his book *Radical Honesty*, Brad Blanton,[7] after asserting that "we all lie like hell. It wears us out. It is the major source of all human stress. Lying kills people," also falls short of recommending that we not lie at all. He fails to recommend a radical policy of truth telling (in spite of the title of his book) because part of our chronic lying, as he sees it, are lies we tell ourselves, something not so easily defined and even less easily stopped. I avoid the self-lying conundrum by defining a lie as a conscious act. Given this definition, lying to ourselves is impossible.

The Truth

By writing about the truth and love of truth, I am letting myself in for a huge philosophical debate which has frozen greater and infinitely more meticulous minds than mine in their tracks.

The idea that truth is something to be discovered with the mind rather than accepted from religion was first recorded in the 4th century BC. It was a result of a new interest in the workings of the physical universe. Socrates and Plato extended their exploration into the realms of ethics, aesthetics, politics and psychology. (Aristotle shifted the emphasis back to empirical inquiry, in defiance of his teacher Plato, who favored speculation and logic with little empirical grounding.) It was the Greek sophists, Plato's contemporaries and intellectual antagonists, who first began to argue that emotion and prejudice are as important as reason in the pursuit of truth. Plato argued for absolute truth, discoverable through a dialogic process which he called dialectic; the sophists believed that opinion, or "doxa," is truth and that truth is wholly relative. Hence Protagoras' famous dictum "Man is the measure of all things."[8]

The dominance of religious truth returned with the Middle Ages, but in the Enlightenment the debate resumed. The Rationalists echoed Plato in arguing that reason is the best guide to truth; the Empiricists, like Aristotle, preferred to rely on the physical facts; the Romantics inadvertently came to parallel the sophists by asserting the importance of emotion and the irrational. (It should be noted that while the sophists were often disingenuous hustlers, the Romantics were earnest seekers rebelling against the excesses of rationalism and industrialization.)

Though Nietzsche was the inheritor of the Romantic tradition from his early idol, Schopenhauer, he was one of the last dewy-eyed thinkers who ever lived. He argued that language (and even thought) are inherently deceptive and that no society can survive without mutually agreed upon falsehoods, ". . . to be truthful means to employ the usual metaphors. Thus, to express it morally, this is the duty to lie according to a fixed convention, to lie with the herd and in a manner binding upon everyone."[9]

Today, those familiar with the work of Nietzsche's inheritors, the structuralist and post-structuralist philosophers, such as Derrida and Foucalt, may sneer at the notion that the concept of truth has any meaning or that it can be discovered.

To my mind, there is nothing that can be called "the truth." The truth changes with time. There are several sometimes seemingly contradictory truths and there is no way to contain the hugely complex facts of nature in any one set of words. But I believe that some statements are truer than others. This book does not propose to have a monopoly on universal moral truths. Instead, it offers a paradigm which, within our culture, has the potential to make our lives happier and richer. What I can say with certainty is that to reap the benefits of practicing Emotional Literacy, one must take "love of truth" seriously and seriously strive to be truthful. Love of truth implies, as George

Sand is believed to have said: "We must accept truth even if it changes our point of view." Being truthful is speaking truth as we understand it. We need to be particularly vigilant within the context of loving, cooperative relationships, where lies often seem necessary to prevent harm, but so often create much more harm than they were intended to avert.

Violence and the Dark Side

Most people have, deep in their hearts, a real need and desire to bond, to be open, loving, and respectful of other's feelings. One of the first tenets of Transactional Analysis is that everyone is born Okay.[10] This idea probably filtered down to Eric Berne from the 19th century philosopher Jean Jacques Rousseau, who maintained that people are born good and it is social ills that make them bad. Philosopher Herbert Marcuse and, initially, Sigmund Freud have called this original goodness the "inborn social instinct" Eros, and the energy that drives it "libido." Freud originally believed that our ability to live harmoniously and lovingly with each other comes from this "Eros principle," while violence and exploitation come from the "ego principle," the side of human nature that is concerned with self-preservation and therefore strives to become as powerful (and therefore safe) as possible and is willing to harm others to achieve its ends.

There are others, like Francis Fukuyama,[11] who have suggested that this Rousseauian conviction that people are intrinsically good while all negativity comes from bad social conditions is a naive, liberal notion. Freud himself in the later part of his life, after witnessing the horrors of WWII, decided that there was, in addition to libido, the life principle, another innate human tendency, an inborn antisocial instinct which he called Thanatos, the Death instinct.

In addition to the positive, cooperative side of people there is a dark side of human nature that we have to reckon with. Beyond the simple lessons of this book we will be confronted with hard situations and, as emotional warriors, we should not be taken by surprise if our efforts are met with hard if not nasty resistance.

The pursuit of Emotional Literacy presupposes that people are born with an innate tendency toward goodness, cooperation, and love; that is, a tendency to exercise ethical power. Without that tendency we would be fighting a constant, exhausting, uphill battle. But we all have forces within that are profoundly unethical, which are not just implanted by a bad culture but are probably innate. These forces involve aggression, greed and unethical manifestations of sexuality. They stem from primitive, irrepressible and even vital and valuable survival instincts.

The moral philosophers of the Enlightenment generally defined evil as error. In the terms of this book, error is equivalent to emotional illiteracy, or a lack of a sense of enlightened self-interest that would make it evident to us that our evil deeds will eventually hurt us by leaving us isolated. But the root of evil may not be just error but the result of deep, instinctive, unchecked survival impulses.

To be an effective emotional warrior you must be able to admit your own aggression, selfishness and greed, your own inborn urge to survive at all costs. You must also be aware of and accept these impulses in others. An Emotional Warrior knows that we all have selfish and aggressive instincts, and managing those instincts in an ethical way is one of the primary aims of emotional wisdom.

Fyodor Dostoyevsky acknowledged this irreducible selfishness in human nature when he wrote:

"To love another as oneself according to Christ's commandment is impossible. Only Christ was able to do this, but Christ is a perpetual and eternal ideal towards which man strives . . ."[12]

There is a dark side, not only to human nature, but also to the human condition. All human beings live every day with the possibility of loss, tragedy, and even disaster.

213

In the modern world we have protected ourselves with technology from many types of tragedy. However, we may have paved the way for a greater collective tragedy—a worldwide catastrophe, for that same technology, if left unchecked, may destroy the biosphere.

The awareness of tragedy is relevant to the pursuit of Emotional Literacy, especially for the emotional warrior. Some survivors of tragedy feel that they no longer have the resources to worry about the rights and needs of others. They may fall into a nihilistic "After all I've been through, I deserve to be happy, by any means necessary" or "I've suffered, why shouldn't others suffer too?" attitude. An emotional warrior must understand this temptation to succumb to the dark side of our nature in response to tragedy, and must be able to resist this temptation. She must understand that she may not be rewarded materially for her efforts, she may even suffer tragedy in spite of her valor; sometimes, tragically, virtue is not only its own reward, but its only reward. A warrior must be prepared for that possibility.

An Emotional Warrior is aware of the dark side, both the dark side of human nature (innate greed and aggression) and the dark side of the human condition (tragedy) and strives to practice honorable ethical power even when one or both of these twin facets of the Dark Side threaten to wreak havoc.

Violence and Abuse

The connection between childhood abuse and violent adult behavior, mediated by emotional numbing, is a strongly-established one.

The relationship is not perfect. There are certain neurological determinants of violent behavior which are strongly associated with trauma to the brain. That is to say, youngsters who experience head injuries, whether accidental or due to abuse, exhibit a certain lack of inhibitory capacity which can result in and is correlated with uncontrolled violent behavior. On the other hand, childhood abuse is also highly correlated with violent adult behavior. In fact, abuse is more strongly correlated with adult violence than brain injury. This underscores the urgent need to stop domestic violence.

The most dangerous mixture of violence determinants is the combination of both abuse and neurological damage.

Using time spent in jail as a rough measure of violent behavior, the results in 95 male juveniles are startling:[13]

No neurological determinants, no abuse **No jail time**
Neurological determinants, no abuse **360 days jail time**
No neurological determinants and abuse **562 days jail time**
Neurological determinants and abuse **1,214 days jail time**

Children with brain injuries almost always incur them from neglect or abuse. Child abuse, especially child abuse that involves blows to the head, is a serious determinant of violent adult behavior. And the trauma of neglect and abuse causes the kind of emotional numbing that makes one capable of abusing or neglecting a child. Intervention and emotional literacy training are desperately needed. By teaching empathy, emotional literacy training stops the vicious cycle of abuse and neglect.

The Critical Parent

Critical thinkers will question the concept of the Critical Parent. Some argue that it is too much like a *homunculus,* a little person inside of our heads. The Critical Parent is just one way to visualize and make accessible a method for decathecting—taking away psychic energy from—a set of recurrent, debilitating prejudiced and deprecatory thoughts. These self-abusive thoughts are not based on the facts of current reality. These thoughts are leftovers from our childhood which distract, demotivate, and demoralize us. The fact that some people hear these as derogatory, insulting, or doom ridden "voices in the head" (what we know as the Critical Parent) makes the process of decathecting and disconnecting from them easier. It is easier because you can speak to, disagree with and evict a voice in your head, whereas it is more difficult to respond to and resist an image or amorphous feeling of inadequacy.

This discussion leads to questions of the validity of the concept of ego states. Are there really three and only three distinct states of the ego which manifest themselves in sequence and which operate in three distinctly different ways?

Again, the value of these concepts is that they help us to better understand human social behavior. They are a useful way of representing human beings in their social transactions. When transactional analysts draw two people with their three ego states on the chalkboard, we know that these are not true representations of these people any more than a street map is a true representation of a city. They are, however, as useful as a street map for getting around in the human situation—that says a great deal for their validity.

---

[1] Nietzsche, Friedrich, *The Genealogy of Morals: An Attack*, written 1887, Anchor Books, Doubleday, 1956.

[2] St. Augustine, "Lying," in *Treatise on Various Subjects*, vol. 14., ed. R. J. Deferrari, Fathers of the Church (Catholic University of America Press, 1952).

[3] Kant, Immanuel. *Critique of Practical Reason and Other Writings in Moral Philosophy* (University of Chicago Press, 1949).

[4] Constant, Benjamin, in *Lying* by Sissela Bok (Vintage, 1978).

[5] De Paulo, Bella M., et al. "Lying in Everyday Life." *Journal of Personality and Social Psychology.* May 1996, v. 70, no. 5.

[6] Bok, Sissela. *Lying* (Vintage, 1978).

[7] Blanton, Brad. *Radical Honesty* (Dell, 1996).

[8] *The Encyclopedia of Philosophy*, Macmillan Publishing Co., Inc. and the Free Press, 1967, p. 505.

[9] Nietzsche, Friedrich, "On Truth and Lies in a Nonmoral Sense," essay written 1873.

[10] Berne, Eric. *What Do You Say After You Say Hello?* (Grove Press, 1976).

[11] Fukuyama, Francis. *The End of History and the Last Man* (The Free Press, 1992).

[12] Dostoyevsky, Fyodor, from his personal diary, April 16, 1864, quoted in *Fyodor Dostoyevsky, A Writer's Life*, Geir Kjetsaa, 1987.

[13] Gladwell, Malcolm. "Damaged." (*New Yorker Magazine*, Feb. 24, 1997).

GLOSSARY

Adult: the rational ego state.

Berne, Eric: the father of Transactional Analysis.

Charisma: the sum total of an individual's personal power.

Child: the creative, aware, spontaneous, intimate ego state. The locus of our emotions.

Critical Parent: a negatively prejudiced Parent ego state. Often heard as a voice that tells us we are not okay; Bad, stupid, ugly, crazy, sick or doomed.

Ego State: one of three separate, coherent ways in which people behave; Parent, Adult or Child.

Emotional awareness: awareness of feelings as opposed to emotional intelligence, a far more complicated skill.

Emotional Intelligence: essentially the same as Emotional Literacy.

Emotional Literacy: a skill that involves understanding our own and other people's emotions as well as knowing how our emotions are best expressed for the maximum enhancement of ethical, personal power.

Emotional Numbing: the complete suppression of the awareness of emotions due, usually, to severe trauma.

Emotional Tone Deafness: the inability to feel certain specific emotions. Similar to color blindness.

Emotional Warrior: an individual who struggles against patriarchic domination with the aim of replacing it with Emotional Literacy in his or her personal life and in society.

Emotions: biochemically based bodily states that affect our behavior.

Empath: a person who is keenly aware of his or her emotions as well as the emotions of others. An empath when not emotionally literate can suffer greatly from his or her heightened awareness.

Empathy: an intuitive capacity to understand emotions.

Existential Payoff: the good feeling that people get from playing a game because the negative payoff confirms an existential position held as part of a script, usually since childhood.

Feelings: same as Emotions.

Game: a series of transactions which fails to accomplish the purpose of getting positive strokes, producing negative strokes instead.

Intuition: a human faculty with which we can sense reality without having to study it.

Love: the master emotion that causes people to play together, be together and work together. The pleasurable feeling of cooperation.

Love of Truth: the eminently human desire to want to understand reality. It implies a willingness to abandon one's beliefs in the face of contradictory information.

Lying: there are two kinds of lies. By commission: saying something that we believe to be false. By omission: failing to say something that we believe another person would want to know.

Negative Stroke: a stroke delivered with a hateful feeling. A stroke that feels bad.

Nurturing Parent: a positively prejudiced Parent ego state.

Paranoia: from the Greek meaning "knowledge on the side." A valid intuitive notion which is however not completely correct.

Paranoid Fantasy: what happens to paranoid knowledge when it is discounted and invalidated. Usually, ideas of being persecuted when we are in the dark about what is going on.

Parent: the prejudging, traditional ego state.

Persecutor: an angry, resentful person who vents his or her feelings on other people.

Positive Stroke: a stroke delivered with a loving feeling. A stroke that feels good.

Psychopath: an antiquated term for an antisocial personality. A person who lacks empathy and is unable to feel emotion.

Rescuer (capitalized): a person who does things he doesn't want to do for other people or who does more than his or her share in any given situation. As opposed to a rescuer (lower case) who helps people in need.

Stroke: an act of social recognition. See also positive stroke.

Stroke City: an exercise to trash the stroke economy.

Stroke Economy: a system of prohibitions about stroking which severely curtails the availability of strokes leading to stroke hunger.

Script: a life plan decided upon early in childhood as a way of coping with the prevailing conditions we live in at the time.

Sympathy: the mental aspect of empathy. The kindly disposed understanding of other people's emotions without an accompanying emotion of one's own.

Transaction: a social exchange of information or strokes.

Transactional Analysis: a system of psychology and psychotherapy which analyzes transactions to understand people.

Truth: an elusive concept. Truth does not exist but it can be approximated. Truth is a belief and we approximate truth when our beliefs reflect the realities of the world. The best approach to truth is the consensus of large numbers of free thinking people.

Truthfulness: speaking what one believes to be the truth.

Victim (capitalized): a person who will not help himself. As opposed to victim (lower case) who is a casualty of bad circumstances.

Window of Opportunity: an optimal period, in early life, in which to learn a certain skill.

REFERENCES

Berne, Eric. *Transactional Analysis in Psychotherapy*. (Grove Press, 1961)

————*Games People Play*. (Grove Press, 1964)

————*Beyond Games and Scripts*. Edited by Claude Steiner (Grove Press, 1976)

Blake, D. D. "Treatment Outcome Research on Post Traumatic Stress Disorder." *CP Clinician Newsletter*. No. 3 (pp. 14–17).

Brom, D., Kleber, R. J., and Defares, P. B. "Brief Psychotherapy for Post Traumatic Stress Disorder." *Journal of Consulting and Clinical Psychology*, 57(5), pp. 607–612.

Eisler Riane. *The Chalice and the Blade*. (HarperCollins, 1988)

Fenestra M., et al. *The Ultimate IQ book*. (Sterling, 1993)

Gilligan, James. *Violence: Our Deadly Epidemic and its Causes*. (Grosset Putnam Books, 1996)

Geller, M. and Ford, Sonna. *Violent Homes Violent Children* (New Jersey Department of Corrections, 1984)

Gladwell, Malcolm. "Damaged. Do new studies of the brain explain why some people turn into violent criminals?" (*The New Yorker*, Feb 24, 1997)

Goleman, Daniel. *Emotional Intelligence*. (Bantam Books, 1996)

Goleman, Daniel. *Vital Lies Simple Truths. The Psychology of Self Deception*. (Touchstone, 1985) [See Part I: "Why dimmed attention soothes pain."]

Gottman, John. *The Heart of Parenting: Raising an Emotionally Intelligent Child*, with a foreword by Daniel Goleman (Simon and Shuster, 1997)

Gray, John. *Men are from Mars: Women are from Venus. A Practical Guide for Improving Communication and Getting What you Want in your Relationships*. (HarperCollins, 1992)

Judith, Anodea. *The Truth about Chacras*. (Llewelyn, 1990)

Laing, Ronald D. *The Politics of the Family*. (Pantheon Books, 1971)

Karpman Stephen. "Fairy Tales and Script Drama Analysis," *Transactional Analysis Bulletin v. 7*, No. 26, April (1968).

Milgram, Stanley. *Obedience to Authority* (Harper and Row, 1974)

Plutchik, Robert. *The Emotions: Facts, Theories and a New Model*. (Random House, 1962)

Salovey, Peter and Mayer, John, D. "Emotional Intelligence," *Imagination Cognition and Personality*. 1989–90 v.9 No. 3, 185.

Stewart, Ian and Joines. *Transactional Analysis Today*. (Lifespace UK, 1989).

Steiner, Claude. *When a Man Loves a Woman; Sexual and Emotional Literacy for Men*. (Grove Press, 1978)

——*TA Made Simple*. (RAPress, 1971)

——*Healing Alcoholism*. (Grove Press, 1979)

——*The Warm Fuzzy Tale*. (Jalmar Press, 1977)

——*Scripts People Live*. (Grove Press, 1974)

——*The Other Side of Power*. (Grove Press, 1981)

——"Transactional Analysis and Emotional Literacy Training." *Transactional Analysis Journal*, January 1996.

Tagney, J. P and Kurt W. Fisher (eds) *Self-conscious Emotions: The Psychology of Shame, Guilt and Pride*. (Guilford, 1995)

Toch, Hans and Kenneth Adams. *The Violent Offender*. (American Psychological Association, 1987)

van der Kohl, Bassel, A., Alexander C. McFarlane, and Lars Weesaeth (eds) *Traumatic Stress* (Guilford, 1996)

INDEX

ABOUT EMOTIONAL LITERACY

Emotional literacy training workshops take place from time to time in different locations in the U.S., Europe, and worldwide.

For emotional literacy literature and training handouts, to get on the mailing list for workshops and training seminars, or for a worldwide directory of emotional warriors, send a self-addressed stamped envelope to:

Emlit
P.O. Box 5224
Berkeley, CA 94705

E-mail us at: emlit@igc.apc.org
Look us up on the web at: www.igc.apc.org/emlit
Send us a fax: (510) 848-9789

ABOUT TRANSACTIONAL ANALYSIS

The International Transactional Analysis Association publishes the quarterly *Transactional Analysis Journal*, a monthly newsletter "The Script," a Transactional Analysis literature database, a directory of members and affiliated organizations around the world, and organizes yearly Transactional Analysis conferences. The ITAA has its headquarters at:

450 Pacific Avenue, Suite 250
San Francisco, CA 94133-4640
Telephone: (510) 989-5640; Fax: (510) 989-9343
e-mail: 76734.2074@compuserve.com
website: www.itaa-net.org

ABOUT THE AUTHOR

Claude Steiner, Ph.D., was born in Paris, France, in 1935. He lived in Spain and Mexico before he came to the U.S. to study engineering and physics. For a while, he made his living as an automobile mechanic. He eventually became a clinical psychologist from the University of Michigan, Ann Arbor. He was a disciple and, later, colleague, friend and collaborator of Eric Berne, the psychiatrist and author of *Games People Play*. With Berne, Steiner was a founding member of The Transactional Analysis Association. After Berne's death in 1971, Dr. Steiner went on to develop the theory and practice of Radical Psychiatry and its corollary Emotional Literacy, which he wrote about extensively in books and journals. He is the author of the ubiquitous fable, *The Warm Fuzzy Tale*.

In the 1980s he took a sabbatical from his practice and traveled in Central America studying propaganda. From 1987 to 1990 he was a senior editor of the quarterly journal *Propaganda Review*. He returned to his practice as a psychologist with an emphasis on Emotional Literacy and the effects, good and bad, of technology on the human spirit. He has three grown children and two grandchildren, and he lives and practices in Berkeley and on his ranch in Mendocino County, California. He still repairs his own cars and ranch machinery. His books include: *Games Alcoholics Play, Scripts People Live, Healing Alcoholism, The Other Side of Power*, and *When a Man Loves a Woman*.